THE SIMPLE ART OF SALT BLOCK COOKING

THE SIMPLE ART OF SALT BLOCK COOKING

GRILL, CURE, BAKE AND SERVE
WITH HIMALAYAN SALT BLOCKS

Jessica Harlan and Kelley Sparwasser

ULYSSES PRESS

Published in the U.S. by:
Ulysses Press
P.O. Box 34402000
Berkeley, CA 94703
www.ulyssespress.com

ISBN13: 978-1-64604-233-3
Library of Congress Control Number: 2015937566

Printed in the United States

10 9 8 7 6 5 4 3 2 1

Acquisitions editor: Casie Vogel
Project editor: Alice Riegert
Managing editor: Claire Chun
Editor: Susan Lang
Proofreader: Renee Rutledge
Cover design: Rebecca Lown
Interior design and layout: what!design @ whatweb.com
Photography: © Judi Swinks Photography; back cover salt block © Alexey Borodin/shutterstock.com
Food stylist: Anna Hartman-Kenzler
Illustrator: Suman Kasturia
Index: Sayre Van Young

IMPORTANT NOTE TO READERS: This book is independently authored and published and no sponsorship or endorsement of this book by, and no affiliation with, any trademarked brands or other products mentioned within is claimed or suggested. All trademarks that appear in this book belong to their respective owners and are used here for informational purposes only. The authors and publisher encourage readers to patronize the quality brands and products mentioned in this book.

For Adam. – KS

For Chip, Sadie, and Gillian – you're the salt to my pepper. –JH

CONTENTS

CHAPTER 4: SEAFOOD MAINS.................. 81

CHAPTER 5: BREADS ON THE BLOCK 97

CHAPTER 6: SWEETS ON SALT.................113

INTRODUCTION

Salt of the earth.
Worth her salt.
Pouring salt in the wound.
Take with a grain of salt.
Back to the salt mines.

It's no coincidence that idioms about salt—both positive and negative—are so pervasive in the English lexicon. After all, salt literally flows through our veins, an essential mineral without which we would perish.

Salt is one of our oldest food seasonings, and was the first preservative enabling humans to survive through scarcity. It's not surprising that its significance led to its use as a currency and a trade commodity (in fact, the word "salary" has its origins in the rations of salt given to soldiers).

While we won't be paying our mortgages with sacks of salt, there's no denying that salt is still integral to our culture, not only as the essential mineral it's always been, but as a cultural phenomenon. Head to the grocery store to refill your saltcellar and you'll choose from table salt, kosher salt, various sea salts, flaky salt, pink salt, black salt, and the list goes on.

Himalayan salt blocks are beautiful, marbled pink slabs of salt carved from deep within the Himalayan mountains in Pakistan. This salt, formed beneath the earth from ancient seabeds and protected for thousands of years by virtue of its inaccessibility, is unadulterated by pollution and other impurities. It contains trace minerals that give it a more complex flavor than standard table or kosher salt, and iron oxide, which lends it a striking pink color.

Because of their high moisture content, salt blocks naturally conduct and retain heat to extreme temperatures, which means they can be heated to a temperature hot enough to cook on, and chilled so they can be used to display and lower the temperature of foods. On the following pages, we'll show you how to use salt blocks on the stove, in the oven, and even on the grill and in the smoker, to create delicious, perfectly seasoned meals.

A TECHNIQUE WORTH MASTERING

We're not going to lie: Cooking with a salt block can be a challenge. Newcomers to this cooking technique might find that a salt block heats unevenly, will crack if it's not heated and cooled just so, and can be a pain to clean and maintain.

So why bother? When you master the art of cooking on a salt block, you'll be richly rewarded. You'll taste the best seared steak of your life. You'll be treated to tender vegetables that are perfectly seasoned. You'll impress dinner guests with stunning presentations.

We liken cooking on a salt block to cooking over a campfire. It takes a while to get started, and the heating is a bit inconsistent and a bit unreliable—but it's a fun, unique way of cooking, and the results are simply delicious!

We'll equip you with the instructions, techniques, and recipes you need to use your salt block to its best advantage. With a little practice and the recipes in this book, you'll soon learn to love cooking on salt blocks as much as we do. It's now the only way we bake flatbread pizzas (see page 101 for our favorite recipes) and one of our preferred ways to cook shrimp (page 82).

So follow along with us and learn how to make a true piece of earth's history into one of your favorite cooking tools.

- Sodium is instrumental in brain function and signals to and from the brain.

- The addition of salt to food enhances flavor by allowing the food to release molecules into the air, boosting the aroma of the food, and therefore how we taste it. Salt also helps to decrease bitter flavors in food.

- The word "salad" is derived from the Latin word for salt ("sal"), because Romans often brined their vegetables.

- Many people believe that Himalayan salt has numerous health benefits, from regulating sleep to preventing varicose veins to acting as an antihistamine. There are even spas that have salt-lined rooms for "salt therapy."

- In the early 1800s in the United States, salt was four times more expensive than beef, since it played an important part in keeping people and livestock alive and healthy.

- Some people swear by a pinch of salt in their coffee grounds before brewing, saying it removes some of the bitter or acidic flavor.

CHOOSING YOUR SALT BLOCK

As ancient as salt blocks are, there are very few offerings in the marketplace and not a lot of variety in terms of size and shape.

The most common salt block is made by California-based **Charcoal Companion**, and it's 12 inches by 8 inches and 1½ inches thick, just big enough to fit over a regular burner. Depending on where you buy it, this same salt block can range in price from $30 to $50, so be sure to shop around for the best price. While we bought ours at Cost Plus World Market, blocks can be found at Crate & Barrel, Home Depot, Sur la Table, Williams-Sonoma, and more.

Another offering is from **Salt Rox**, based in Kentucky. Founder John Tucker has developed a proprietary technique to treat his salt blocks so they are more durable and can be brought to temperature more quickly without breaking. The company's salt blocks are 2 inches thick and come in various sizes. The company also offers serving plates, shot glasses, and bowls made of salt, as well as granules of salt for seasoning.

Whatever brand you choose, make sure that salt blocks used for cooking are at least 1 inch thick, preferably 1½ to 2 inches. Square salt blocks will fit over your burner better, offering slightly more even heating but less cooking surface, whereas rectangular blocks will be cooler on the part of the block that is farthest from the heat source. If you intend to use a salt block only for chilling or room temperature use, a thinner version is fine.

A good source to visit online (or in person, if you're lucky enough to be in the area) is **The Meadow**, which has stores in Portland, Oregon, and New York City. This store has the most definitive assortment of salt blocks and other Himalayan salt products. Within the salt block category at The Meadow, there are two different grades of quality: The cookware grade blocks are intended for home use, while the professional grade blocks are more durable against breakage due to changes in temperature, and are even guaranteed against breakage for the first three uses. Owner Mark Bitterman is one of the leading experts on salt and has written two cookbooks about salt and cooking with salt blocks.

THE SALT BLOCK KITCHEN: OUR MOST ESSENTIAL TOOLS

We recommend having on hand a number of tools to make cooking with and maintaining your salt block a lot easier.

DIGITAL LASER THERMOMETER: This type of thermometer uses a laser to instantly check the surface temperature. It is essential for monitoring the temperature of your salt block so you'll know when it has reached the appropriate cooking temperature. You can also use it to check the variation of temperature on the entire surface of the block and to identify the hottest and coolest parts of the cooking surface. Of all the tools we recommend in this section, we think this is the most essential.

SALT BLOCK HOLDER: Some manufacturers make a metal frame to accommodate their salt blocks. This frame has handles on either side, which makes it easier to lift and move your salt block, especially if it is hot or if you're moving it into or out of the oven. The holder is also handy if your block is cracked or even broken in half, as it will hold it together so you can still use it.

SILICONE OVEN MITTS: We've been able to heat our salt blocks to temperatures of 500°F to 600°F, especially on the grill. You won't want to lift a salt block with just any oven mitt when it's that hot! Silicone oven mitts are the best we've found to protect hands from extreme heat, and their rubbery surface ensures a secure grip on the block. An alternative is a pair of welding gloves, which are designed to be used when handling red-hot metal.

METAL SPATULA: A slotted fish spatula or other metal spatula is a good option for flipping and lifting foods from your salt block. You don't need to worry about protecting the surface of the block as you do with nonstick-coated or enamel-coated pans, and the sturdy metal can loosen food that is stuck or scrape burnt-on residue when cleaning.

RAZOR BLADE SCRAPER: For removing stuck-on bits, we find that a razor blade scraper from a hardware store is very effective. Don't raid your toolbox; buy one just for kitchen use.

STIFF CLEANING BRUSH: Look in the cleaning section of your supermarket or hardware store for a small brush with the stiffest, roughest bristles you can find. It's ideal for scrubbing the surface of your salt block for cleaning.

USING YOUR SALT BLOCK

The first thing to know about salt blocks is that they need to be heated slowly and gradually. Because the inside of the block contains moisture, heating the block too quickly can cause it to crack or even explode.

You might be concerned that the heating time for a salt block isn't worth the wait, and that it'll prolong getting dinner on the table. But heating a salt block doesn't take much longer than preheating an oven.

When we cook on our salt blocks, the first thing we do when we enter the kitchen is to put the blocks on the stove and start heating them. Only then do we get out ingredients and begin prepping. We've found that by the time we have all of our ingredients ready to go, the salt block is hot enough to use. That's why the first instruction for just about every recipe in this book is to preheat your salt block.

Stovetop Use

The best type of stove for salt block cooking is one with gas burners.

The first few times you use a salt block, you should take extra care and allow more time for heating. Center the salt block on the burner, and set the heat on low. After about 15 minutes, increase the heat to medium-low, then after another 15 minutes to medium. Continue heating gradually, increasing the heat incrementally as needed and checking with your laser thermometer until you reach the desired temperature. It should take about 45 minutes of gradual heating to reach the proper temperature.

If you use a salt block on an electric stove with either a glass top or burner coils, you will need a silicone pie crust shield and a round tart pan with a removable bottom that's bigger than your burner. Place the silicone pie crust shield on the glass or around the coils of a small burner to protect the surface of your stove, and then remove the bottom of the tart pan and invert just the ring and place it on the pie crust shield, being careful not to touch the burner itself. Set the salt block on top of the tart pan ring and begin the heating process. A salt block cannot be used on an induction cooktop.

After you've used your salt block three or four times, you can reduce the amount of time between heat increases so that the entire heating process takes around 30 minutes.

Oven Use

If you are using your salt block in the oven, do NOT heat it there, as it has been reported that it may explode! Instead, preheat the oven to the proper temperature and, as the oven heats, heat the salt block on the stove as instructed in Stovetop Use (page 6). When the salt block is within 25°F of the appropriate cooking temperature and the oven is preheated, you can transfer it to the oven to continue heating. Some recipes in this book call for the food to be placed on the preheated salt block before transferring it to the oven, or you can remove it from the oven to add the food, then return it to the oven to cook.

Note: If the salt block is hot enough, foods like meats, seafood, and doughs will form a seared crust and will release easily from the salt block after a few moments, just as they do on uncoated stainless steel. But for some foods, such as the moist dough in Chewy Bagel Bites (page 98) or the fried egg in Salt-Fried Egg in the Hole (page 68), we recommend brushing a bit of oil on the salt block to make the surface more nonstick. The best oils to use are ones with a high smoke point so they won't scorch. We recommend grapeseed oil, peanut oil, canola oil, or ghee (clarified butter).

Grill Use

Salt blocks are great on the grills because you can sear proteins at very high heat without having to worry about flare-ups. We tried recipes on gas, charcoal, and pellet grills, and the blocks performed beautifully. A charcoal cooker like the Big Green Egg allows you the option of both direct and indirect cooking.

- Treat your gas and pellet grills exactly as you would a stovetop. Put the salt block on the cold grill, start the gas on low with the lid closed, and gently raise the heat until the salt block reaches the desired temperature.

- To heat a salt block on a charcoal grill, put hot coals on one side of the grill and the block on the opposite side to protect it from direct exposure to flame. We actually prefer building a big fire in the center of the grill while simultaneously heating the block on the gas stovetop in the block holder and then transferring it to the grill at around 400°F. It is easier to regulate the block's warming temperature, and you don't have to refresh the coals midway or remove the grill grate to spread the coals around.

In our experience, 400°F is an acceptable point not to worry about direct flame from the gas or charcoal, and we can then take the block up to as hot as 600°F.

Chilling the Salt Block

A salt block can also be chilled to use in preparing or presenting cold foods, such as Salmon Avocado Sushi (page 84) and Green Chile Guacamole (page 26). To chill the salt block, place it in the refrigerator for at least 3 hours or overnight. It will chill to a temperature of 40°F or less, depending on the length of time it spends in the refrigerator and how cold your refrigerator is. Remove the salt block from the refrigerator when ready to use, and place it on a trivet or a clean dishtowel to protect surfaces, as it might "sweat," which can harm surfaces. We recommend investing in a separate salt block just for chilling, so that it will stay pristine and will make the best presentation.

Note: We do not recommend putting a salt block in the freezer. While freezing will not damage your salt block, we found that it causes the block to sweat too much as it comes to room temperature, which makes the food on the block overly salty for cold food presentations.

BUT WON'T MY FOOD BE TOO SALTY?

A common concern is that food will end up unbearably salty when cooked on a pure salt surface. And if you don't use the salt block the right way, overly salty food is a likelihood. During our recipe testing, there were plenty of times we had to scrap a finished dish because it was way too salty. But in other cases, we were pleasantly surprised to discover that there was virtually no salt taste—in fact, we needed to add a bit of seasoning!

Here are the things we found that cause a dish to be too salty:

SALT BLOCK IS NOT HOT ENOUGH: If the salt block is not hot enough, the food you are cooking won't sear quickly enough and will require more cooking time on the block, which allows more time for salt to be absorbed into the food. Make sure your cooking surface is at least 300°F before you add the food. That way the exterior of the food will quickly sear and seal.

FOOD HAS A HIGH MOISTURE CONTENT: The wetter the food, the more it will dissolve the surface of the salt block, which causes more salt to adhere to the food. Some examples of foods that can get too salty: greens that give off liquid when cooking; the cut surfaces of vegetables, such as zucchini or brussels sprouts; and, on cold surfaces, high-moisture foods like cucumbers and juicy fruits. For all of these foods, try to limit the surface that comes in contact with the salt block. You can do this by stacking or fanning the food, or placing garnishes like a bundle of leafy herbs underneath the food. If just a small portion of the food is exposed to the salt, it'll be just enough salt to season the whole thing. You can also stir the food before serving so that saltier bits mix into the less seasoned parts.

FOOD HAS BEEN ON THE SALT BLOCK FOR TOO LONG: If you're using the salt block for a presentation, be sure that the food will be eaten quickly, as the longer food is on a chilled or room-temperature salt block, the more salt it will absorb.

For presentation of creamy dishes like Edamame "Hummus" (page 30), Green Chile Guacamole (page 26), or Salted Butterscotch Pudding (page 121), put thick dollops on the salt block. When taking a serving, give the food a stir on the plate before eating, to distribute the salt evenly.

CLEANING AND CARING FOR YOUR SALT BLOCK

Right out of the package, your new salt block is gorgeous: a glowing slab of pale pink marbled salt. If you use it a lot, it won't stay that way for long—but that's okay! Salt blocks are meant to be used and enjoyed, and when yours cracks or the block becomes too damaged, it's time to invest in a new one.

Still, here's how to prolong its life:

Cooling the Salt Block

When you are finished cooking on a salt block, remove it from the hot burner to another burner or a cooling rack, or leave it to cool right on the burner for about 20 to 30 minutes before moving it to a cooling rack or a trivet. If you try to clean it before it's cool, a sudden change in temperature might cause it to crack. You should, however, use a metal spatula or paint scraper to scrape off stuck-on bits of food while the salt block is still hot.

Washing the Salt Block

Unless there is residue stuck onto your salt block, you don't necessarily need to wash it. Instead you could use a dry, stiff brush to scrape away any caked-on food. If you feel like you need to wash the salt block, no soap or detergent is needed. Rinse it under warm running water (hold it upright in the sink so it isn't submerged), and use a scraper or a stiff, wet brush to work off burnt bits or discolorations. Wipe with a wet dishcloth to remove any excess loose sediment. The salt block will dissolve gradually, which is expected and unavoidable. Washing it only when needed will prolong its life.

To clean a salt block that was used for chilling, either rinse off the block if there's stuck-on food or simply wipe it down with a damp dishcloth.

Place the salt block to dry on a cooling rack set over a dishtowel or a baking sheet, and use a clean towel to pat the top of the block dry. Let it dry for 24 hours before using it again.

Note: Do NOT place a salt block in the dishwasher as it will dissolve completely.

Storing the Salt Block

Humidity and moisture will cause the salt block to sweat, which dissolves the salt, so store it in a dry place, such as a cabinet.

Designating Salt Blocks

If you plan on multiple uses for a salt block, consider buying several blocks. We have one or two blocks designated for cooking, one for baking, and one for chilling. This avoids flavor transfer and keeps the salt block you use for chilled presentations looking nice.

CHAPTER 1

APPETIZERS

Whether using a salt block hot or chilled, serving up appetizers on it makes for an impressive and interactive presentation at your next party. We developed these recipes with entertaining in mind—they all make ideal dishes for a cocktail party, sit-down dinner, or some occasion in between!

HERBED PANCAKES WITH CURED SALMON AND CRÈME FRAÎCHE

These savory pancakes are a nod to one of our favorite Russian-inspired appetizers, blini. They make an elegant appetizer for a party, but we could make a meal out of them with a green salad on the side. We like to keep tubes of dill paste, found in the produce section of the supermarket, on hand for this recipe.

MAKES 18 TO 20 PANCAKES

¾ cup all-purpose flour

¾ cup whole wheat flour

2 teaspoons baking powder

1 teaspoon kosher salt

1 cup buttermilk

2 large eggs

½ stick unsalted butter, melted and cooled slightly

1 tablespoon minced fresh dill or dill paste, plus more for garnish

grapeseed or canola oil

2 ounces cured salmon

½ cup crème fraîche

1 Preheat the salt block on the stove, beginning with low heat and gradually increasing the temperature to medium-high, until the surface temperature is 375°F.

2 Meanwhile, prepare the pancake batter. With a whisk, combine the all-purpose flour, whole wheat flour, baking powder, and salt in a medium mixing bowl. In another medium bowl, whisk together the buttermilk, eggs, and melted butter. Add the dry ingredients to the wet ingredients, and stir with the whisk just until smooth and well combined. The batter will be thick. Stir in the dill.

3 Brush the hot salt block lightly with grapeseed or canola oil. Drop batter by the heaping tablespoon, spreading it out slightly to make pancakes around 2 inches wide. Let cook for about 5 minutes, until the underside is browned, then flip using a metal spatula, such as a fish spatula. The pancakes might stick slightly but should release when dislodged with the metal spatula. Cook for another 1 to 2 minutes until the other side is browned. Continue with the remaining batter, brushing more oil on the block if needed. Keep cooked pancakes warm in a 170°F oven or under a clean dishtowel.

4 To serve, top each pancake with a small piece of salmon and a small dollop of crème fraîche. Garnish with a sprig of fresh dill.

COOK'S NOTE

Since the part of the block that is directly over the heat source is hotter than the sides, make sure to use a laser thermometer to gauge the temperature in various parts of the block and check the pancakes on the hottest part first, as they will likely cook faster.

SWEET POTATO CHIPS

Sweet potato chips are a deliciously addictive snack on their own, but also make a great accompaniment to Beef Carpaccio (see page 32). Our version picks up just the right amount of salt and has a nice crunch.

MAKES ABOUT 20 CHIPS

1 large sweet potato, (about 10 ounces)   ¼ cup melted ghee

1 Preheat the oven to 350°F. Preheat two salt blocks on the stove, beginning with low heat and gradually increasing the temperature to medium-high, until the surface temperature is about 350°F. Transfer the hot salt blocks to the middle rack in the oven.

2 Peel the sweet potato, and cut into ⅛-inch-thick slices with a mandolin. Brush the sweet potato slices on both sides with melted ghee. Place on one of the hot salt blocks, and set the second hot salt block on top. Bake in the oven for 10 to 12 minutes until the chips are crisp. Work in batches to cook all the slices. Allow to cool before eating.

COOK'S NOTE

Make sure the sweet potato slices are well coated with ghee to prevent them from sticking to the two salt blocks needed for this recipe. Once the sugar in the sweet potatoes begins to brown, it will burn quickly, so set a timer. Use caution when you place and remove the second salt block, which sits on top of the first block.

BEEF NEGAMAKI

This Japanese sushi-house appetizer is a favorite of Jessica's husband. It's basically beef wrapped around scallions and grilled or sautéed. Usually the beef is marinated in a salty-sweet sauce, but this recipe calls for a sauce to drizzle over the cooked negamaki.

MAKES 12 PIECES

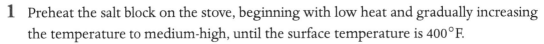

For the Beef
2 petite sirloin steaks (about 6 ounces each), trimmed of excess fat

2 scallions

For the Sauce
¼ cup plus 1 teaspoon ponzu sauce, divided

¼ cup rice vinegar

¼ teaspoon toasted sesame oil

½ teaspoon cornstarch

1 scallion, light green part only, minced

1   Preheat the salt block on the stove, beginning with low heat and gradually increasing the temperature to medium-high, until the surface temperature is 400°F.

2   Meanwhile, place the steak between two pieces of plastic wrap or parchment paper. Using a meat mallet, pound the steak into a rough rectangular shape, about ⅛ inch thick or less. Trim the white end from each of the two scallions to leave a piece that is just slightly longer than the widest part of each piece of meat. Slice the two scallion segments lengthwise into several long, thin strips. Arrange the strips across the wide end of each steak and roll tightly, jelly roll style. Tie pieces of butcher string to hold the roll closed at either end, as well as in one or two places in the middle. Wrap in plastic wrap, and refrigerate until ready to cook.

3   To make the sauce, combine ¼ cup of the ponzu sauce with the rice vinegar and sesame oil in a small saucepan over medium heat. In a small bowl, mix together the cornstarch and the remaining 1 teaspoon of ponzu sauce. When the ponzu and vinegar mixture simmers, whisk in the cornstarch mixture. Cook, whisking constantly, for 1 minute or until the mixture thickens slightly. Stir in the minced scallion, and set aside.

4   When the salt block reaches temperature, unwrap the beef and place the two rolls on the hot block. Cook, turning every 2 to 3 minutes, until evenly browned, about 6 to 8 minutes total. Remove from the block and let cool for 5 minutes. Remove the strings and slice crosswise into 1-inch pieces. Arrange on a platter and drizzle with the sauce. Serve warm.

BALSAMIC ROASTED TOFU WITH TOMATOES AND BASIL

Vegetarians and vegans will love this easy appetizer, which is a great fresh option for the summer. You can even make it on the grill if you want a smoky flavor.

MAKES 24 PIECES

1 block extra firm tofu

¼ cup plus 1 tablespoon balsamic vinegar, divided

1 tablespoon extra virgin olive oil

sea salt

12 cherry tomatoes, halved

24 fresh basil leaves

1 Preheat the oven to 350°F. Preheat the salt block on the stove, beginning with low heat and gradually increasing the temperature to medium-high, until the surface temperature is 350°F to 375°F. Transfer the hot salt block to the middle rack in the oven.

2 Press the tofu using a tofu press or a plate weighted with a food can or two, to release excess liquid. Halve the tofu horizontally and cut into cubes. Place in a bowl, toss with ¼ cup of the vinegar and the olive oil, and let sit for 30 minutes. Remove with a slotted spoon to a paper towel, and blot dry. Take the hot salt block out of the oven, and arrange the tofu pieces on the block. They should sizzle when they come in contact with the block.

3 Return the salt block to the oven and cook for 30 minutes, turning the tofu pieces halfway through cooking, until they have a chewy texture and crisp edges. Transfer to a bowl, and drizzle with the remaining 1 tablespoon of vinegar. Season with sea salt to taste.

4 On each of 24 toothpicks or short skewers, place a tomato half, a piece of basil, and a piece of tofu. Serve at room temperature.

TUNA TARTARE WITH SESAME WONTON CHIPS

Tuna tartare is a staple on many restaurant menus for good reason. It's simple to make, but is certain to impress your guests. We lightly dress the tuna to enhance its taste without masking the rich flavor of the fish.

SERVES 2

12 fresh wonton wrappers, cut in half diagonally

½ cup sesame oil

3 teaspoons ponzu sauce

1 teaspoon fresh lime juice

½ pound sushi-grade tuna, diced into ¼-inch pieces

½ scallion, thinly sliced on the bias

½ teaspoon minced cilantro

½ teaspoon minced fresh ginger

¼ teaspoon lime zest

½ ripe, large avocado, diced

black sesame seeds

For the Sesame Wonton Chips

1 Preheat the oven to 400°F. Preheat the salt block on the stove, beginning with low heat and gradually increasing the temperature to medium-high, until the surface temperature is 350°F to 375°F. Transfer the hot salt block to the middle rack in the oven.

2 Liberally brush both sides of 12 wonton halves with sesame oil, and carefully lay the triangles flat on the hot salt block. Bake for 4½ to 5 minutes until golden brown. Remove the chips from the salt block, using a metal spatula if necessary to dislodge any that may have stuck to the block. Repeat with the remaining 12 wonton triangles.

For the Tuna Tartare

1 Chill a salt block in the refrigerator for several hours or overnight.

2 In a medium bowl, combine the ponzu sauce and lime juice. Add the tuna, and toss to coat. Add the scallion, cilantro, ginger, and lime zest, and stir to combine. Gently fold in the avocado.

3 To serve, turn the tartare onto the chilled salt block, and garnish with a sprinkling of black sesame seeds on top. Use the wonton chips to scoop and eat the tartare.

COOK'S NOTE

When making these wonton chips you want to be *very* generous in applying sesame oil. The chips will stick to the salt block if they are only lightly coated with oil. Watch them closely after 4 minutes of baking as they quickly turn from golden and toasted to dark brown and unpleasant on the palate. The chips will keep for a couple of days stored at room temperature in an airtight container.

ROASTED EDAMAME

Tender and toothsome, these edamame make a great snack or addition to a party. Ingredients such as the nori (dried seaweed), Sichuan peppercorns, and black sesame seeds may all be readily found in Asian grocery stores. You can make the seaweed mixture in advance and store it in a spice jar.

SERVES 2 TO 4

1 sheet nori

¼ teaspoon Sichuan peppercorns

¼ teaspoon dried orange peel

¼ teaspoon dried ginger

1 teaspoon black sesame seeds

¼ teaspoon dried garlic

1 (8-ounce) package frozen shelled edamame, thawed

1 tablespoon extra virgin olive oil

1 Preheat the oven to 400°F. Preheat the salt block on the stove, beginning with low heat and gradually increasing the temperature to medium-high, until the surface temperature is 400F° to 425°F. Transfer the hot salt block to the middle rack in the oven.

2 Make the seaweed mixture. Break up the sheet of dried seaweed into a spice grinder. Grind for about 10 seconds, until the seaweed is a powder. Add the peppercorns, dried orange peel, dried ginger, black sesame seeds, and dried garlic to the spice grinder, and pulse about 10 times to combine. Set aside.

3 Place the edamame in a colander, rinse with cold water, shake off excess water, and pat dry with a paper towel. Transfer to a medium bowl, and toss with the olive oil. Add 1 tablespoon of the seaweed mixture, and toss to coat. Feel free to add more seaweed mixture as desired.

4 Spread the edamame on the hot salt block, being cautious not to burn yourself. Roast for 20 minutes, carefully turning after approximately 10 minutes. Serve warm.

COOK'S NOTE

You will have seaweed mixture left over, so use it to make a compound butter to serve over baked chicken or fish, sprinkle over stir-fried vegetables, or toss with rice for a simple side dish.

SCALLOP AND SHRIMP CEVICHE

This vibrant presentation of ceviche will impress friends and family not only for its beauty, but for its bright flavors. The acid from the lime juice "cooks" the seafood in this dish. It is important to purchase very fresh sea scallops and shrimp, and to plan ahead since you must marinate the seafood in the lime juice for at least 6 to 8 hours before serving.

SERVES 4 TO 6

4 large sea scallops, foot removed

1 cup lime juice, divided

⅓ pound large shrimp, peeled and deveined

½ heart of palm

½ medium avocado, diced into ¼-inch pieces

1 tablespoon minced red bell pepper

1 scallion, thinly sliced on the bias

1 tablespoon minced cilantro

½ teaspoon minced jalapeño (optional)

¼ teaspoon chili powder

½ lime, cut into wedges

1 Chill a salt block in the refrigerator for several hours or overnight.

2 Slice each scallop into three equally thick disks and place in a small bowl. Add just enough lime juice to cover, approximately ⅓ cup. Cover the bowl with plastic wrap, and refrigerate for at least 6 to 8 hours and up to 24 hours.

3 Cut each shrimp in half lengthwise and then in thirds, and place in a medium glass bowl. Add just enough lime juice to cover, approximately ⅔ cup. Cover the bowl with plastic wrap, and refrigerate for at least 6 to 8 hours and up to 24 hours.

4 Remove the scallops from the juice, pat dry with a paper towel, and refrigerate. Drain the shrimp in a colander, pressing out as much of the excess juice as possible. Leave the shrimp in the colander so that lime juice can continue to drain, then lightly pat with a paper towel and refrigerate.

5 Cut the heart of palm in half, lengthwise, and then into ¼-inch thick half moons. Begin arranging the scallops, shrimp, and heart of palm on the chilled salt block. Scatter the avocado, bell pepper, scallion, cilantro, and jalapeño, if using, evenly over the top. The block should be completely covered. Sprinkle the chili powder over the top, and serve immediately with lime wedges on the side.

SHRIMP SALAD IN CUCUMBER CUPS

This elegant appetizer is a wonderfully easy dish for a baby shower, garden party, or other spring or summer occasion. To make the recipe even easier, we buy the smallest size frozen shrimp that are already cooked, peeled, and cleaned, and we often use the prepared dill paste that comes in a tube.

MAKES ABOUT 20 PIECES

2 cups cooked shrimp, roughly chopped

⅓ cup mayonnaise

2 tablespoons sour cream

1 tablespoon minced fresh dill or dill paste

2 teaspoons fresh lemon juice, plus more for drizzling

1 English cucumber

1   Chill the salt block in the refrigerator for several hours.

2   In a medium bowl, stir together the shrimp, mayonnaise, sour cream, dill, and 2 teaspoons of lemon juice.

3   Peel the cucumber (or leave on "stripes" of peel lengthwise for a decorative look). Slice off and discard the ends, then cut the cucumber crosswise into 1-inch pieces. Use a melon baller or a round teaspoon to scoop a little indentation into the cut side of each cucumber slice. Spoon a little of the shrimp salad into each indentation and arrange on the chilled salt block. Drizzle with the remaining lemon juice. Serve immediately.

GREEN CHILE GUACAMOLE

One of Jessica's favorite restaurants in the world is Gabriel's outside of Santa Fe, New Mexico. One of the attractions is the guacamole, which is made tableside. It's theatrical and fun, and you can tell the server exactly how you like your guac, whether you want extra spice, no onions, or another squeeze of lime.

This recipe is similar. It's a fun dish to serve at your next party, particularly if you wait until the guests arrive to make it. A flat wooden spatula is ideal for preparing this recipe — it can mash and scrape to create the perfect consistency and integrate just the right amount of salt.

SERVES 6 TO 8

3 medium avocados

½ lime, juiced

½ teaspoon garlic powder

¼ cup minced cilantro

2 tablespoons diced canned green chiles, drained

1 Chill the salt block in the refrigerator for several hours.

2 When the salt block is chilled, halve the avocados and use a spoon to scoop the flesh onto the block. Squeeze the lime juice over the avocados, and sprinkle on the garlic powder, cilantro, and green chiles. Use a flat wooden spatula to chop and mash the avocado, scraping it into a mound, then mashing it again. Continue working the mixture until the ingredients are well combined, the texture is to your liking, and the salt has adequately seasoned the mixture.

3 Transfer the guacamole to a serving bowl or serve as is (see cook's note).

COOK'S NOTE

Once you mix the guacamole to your liking, you can move it to a serving dish to keep it from getting too salty. If you plan to serve it on the salt block, mound it in the center of the block and show your guests how to scoop up a dollop that combines guacamole from the top and from the bottom, where the guacamole has been in contact with the block. Or, if the guacamole will be sitting on the block for a while, layer some romaine lettuce leaves underneath the guacamole after you've mashed it to your liking.

CHEESE PLATE WITH CONDIMENTS

A salt block can be the basis for a stunning cheese display. We love to put together a carefully selected array of three cheeses on a block, with two or three complementary condiments. Leave the cheese in wedges or overlap or fan to limit contact with the block. For the best results, follow these tips:

- Chill the salt block in the refrigerator for several hours or overnight.

- If slicing, overlap or fan the slices so that only a small part of each slice is in contact with the salt block.

- Place liquid condiments and mustard in small, clear glass bowls. Mound thicker condiments, like chutney or jam, directly on the salt block.

TRY THESE COMBINATIONS

Soft Cheese Trio:

Brie, Humboldt Fog, chèvre

Condiment ideas: pepper jelly, honey, pear slices

Sheep's Milk:

Manchego, Camembert, Idizabal

Condiment ideas: quince paste, dried figs, Marcona almonds

Bold Trio:

Truffle Tremor, sharp cheddar, Cayuga Blue

Condiment ideas: honey, chutney, Granny Smith apple slices

Italian Cheeses:

Burrata, La Tur, Piave Vecchio

Condiment ideas: dried cherries, mostarda (a sweet and spicy Italian condiment made of candied fruit in a mustard-flavored sauce), fig jam

Blue Cheese Plate:

Gorgonzola Dolce, Point Reyes Original Blue, Cashel Blue

Condiment ideas: fig preserve, truffled honey, caramelized onions

CHARCUTERIE PLATE WITH CONDIMENTS

A salt block can beautifully present charcuterie, just as it does cheese. You will need to be more mindful of how you display the meats since many already have salt in their cures. We like to use small squares of butcher paper or even slate cocktail coasters for a stunning contrast of colors for the charcuterie display. Try serving fresh bread and good crackers with each of these plates, and cheese is always a good accompaniment. Follow the same tips as given for the Cheese Plate with Condiments (page 27) to turn your salt block into a functional display.

TRY THESE COMBINATIONS

Basic Trio:

Prosciutto, country pâté, chicken liver mousse

Condiment ideas: sliced apples and figs

Spanish Ham Duo:

Iberico and Serrano hams

Condiment ideas: Marcona almonds and melon

Italian Charcuterie Plate:

Bresaola, Genoa salami, capicola

Condiment ideas: giardiniera and marinated piquanté peppers

Three Little Pigs:

Speck, mortadella, pork rillette

Condiment ideas: caperberry and grainy mustard

Hot, Hot, Hot:

Soppressata, spicy chorizo, spicy salami

Condiment ideas: cornichon and olives

EDAMAME "HUMMUS"

Chef Linton Hopkins, of Restaurant Eugene in Atlanta, makes a cashew mayonnaise from soaked cashews that is insanely addictive. We've adapted the technique for this recipe, which is the perfect complement to vegetable crudités such as snap peas, celery, and red bell pepper.

SERVES 6 TO 8

½ cup raw cashews

1 (8-ounce) package frozen shelled edamame, thawed

4 cups water

2 tablespoons fresh lemon juice

¼ cup peanut oil

1 teaspoon minced fresh mint

1 Place the cashews in a small bowl, and cover with water. Soak overnight, then drain the cashews, and set aside.

2 Chill a salt block in the refrigerator for several hours or overnight.

3 In a medium saucepan over medium-high heat, bring the edamame and 4 cups of water to a boil. Cook until mushy, about 10 to 15 minutes. Strain, rinse with cold water, and shake off excess moisture before placing on a clean dishtowel. Gently rub the edamame with the towel to loosen the skins. Remove as many of the skins as possible for a smoother dip.

4 Add the cashews and edamame to the bowl of a food processor. Process for 1 minute. Scrape the sides of the bowl, and add the lemon juice. Process until smooth, about 1 to 1½ minutes.

5 While the food processor is running, add the peanut oil through the feed tube. Continue to process until silky, about 1 to 2 minutes.

6 Transfer to the chilled salt block, and sprinkle mint over the top. Using a spatula, work the dip over the salt block until the mint is incorporated and the "hummus" is lightly salted, about 30 seconds. Transfer to a serving bowl and serve chilled or at room temperature.

Continue working the dip over the salt block until salted to taste if you want it more than lightly salted. The flavors develop as this dip sits, so make it a day ahead of the party. To store, cover with plastic wrap directly on top of the "hummus" to prevent a dry layer of skin from forming.

BEEF CARPACCIO

Use fresh, quality beef for this recipe as you are consuming it raw. Freezing the tenderloin makes it much easier to slice thinly. We suggest grating Salt-Cured Egg Yolks (page 63) over the top as a garnish and serving Sweet Potato Chips (page 17) on the side.

SERVES 2

¼ pound beef tenderloin, frozen 2 hours

1 cup fresh, whole Italian parsley leaves

½ small shallot, peeled and thinly sliced

½ tablespoon capers, chopped

½ teaspoon fresh lemon juice

1 teaspoon extra virgin olive oil

½ teaspoon Dijon mustard

Worcestershire sauce

freshly cracked black pepper

1 Chill a salt block in the refrigerator for several hours or overnight.

2 Thinly slice the beef tenderloin, and lay the slices out side by side between two pieces of plastic wrap, forming a rectangle. Using the flat side of a meat mallet, pound out the slices paper-thin. Set aside in the refrigerator.

3 In a small bowl, add the parsley, shallot, capers, lemon juice, and olive oil, and toss to combine.

4 Arrange the beef on the salt block. Scatter small dollops of mustard on the beef and top with a couple of dashes of Worcestershire sauce. Top with the parsley mixture and a few turns of freshly cracked pepper. Serve immediately.

GOAT CHEESE AND CHIVE GOUGÈRES

A *gougère* is a classic French savory pastry that is meant to be eaten right out of the oven while it's piping hot. They're one of our favorite things to make for company (the dough can be made ahead of time and stored in the refrigerator), and they always elicit rave reviews. A word of caution: They're addictive!

MAKES ABOUT 3 DOZEN

1 cup water

½ stick unsalted butter

¼ teaspoon kosher salt

1 cup all-purpose flour

4 large eggs, room temperature

10 ounces soft goat cheese (chèvre)

⅓ cup finely grated Parmesan cheese, plus more for sprinkling

2 tablespoons minced fresh chives

freshly ground pepper

1   Preheat the oven to 350°F. Preheat the salt block on the stove, beginning with low heat and gradually increasing the temperature to medium-high, until the surface temperature is 350°F to 375°F. Transfer the hot salt block to the middle rack in the oven.

2   Meanwhile, make the dough. In a medium saucepan, combine the water, butter, and salt. Bring to a boil over medium heat, stirring occasionally until the butter melts. Add the flour all at once and cook, stirring constantly, until the flour and liquid form a smooth, thick dough. Continue stirring and pressing the dough against the bottom of the saucepan to cook off more of the liquid, 1 to 2 minutes more.

3   Transfer the dough to a stand mixer fitted with a paddle attachment, and mix at low speed for several minutes, until the dough stops steaming. Add the eggs, one at a time, mixing after every addition until the egg is well incorporated into the dough. Beat in the goat cheese, ⅓ cup of Parmesan cheese, and the freshly ground pepper.

4   Spoon the dough into a pastry bag fitted with a large, round tip. Remove the salt block from the oven, placing it on a burner or a trivet. Quickly pipe mounds of dough onto the block, about 1 inch in height and diameter, leaving an inch or two between mounds. Sprinkle the top of each with a pinch of Parmesan cheese.

5   Return the salt block to the oven, and cook for 20 to 25 minutes, until the gougères are golden brown. Do not open the oven for the first 10 minutes of cooking or the gougères will not puff as much. Serve warm or at room temperature.

CHAPTER 2

VEGETABLES

Just about any vegetable can benefit from a hint of salt to bring out its sweetness and earthiness. And a hot salt block is an ideal cooking vessel to sear vegetables. Just be mindful that vegetables with a high water content, such as zucchini, greens, and tomatoes, have the potential to become overly salty if they wilt and release water on the salt block, causing the salt to dissolve. To avoid this, try cooking so the rind or skin, rather than a cut surface, is in contact with the block, and don't leave the vegetables in contact with the salt for very long.

WILD MUSHROOM AND GOAT CHEESE BEGGAR'S PURSES

Vegetarians will appreciate the elegant presentation of these little pouches of mushrooms and creamy cheese — one or two makes an ideal main course for a meatless meal. Individually, they are a nice side dish or appetizer. Working with phyllo dough is a labor-intensive and exacting process, but if you follow our instructions you'll have no problem creating these pastries.

MAKES 6 PURSES

1 tablespoon unsalted butter

12 ounces mixed mushrooms, cut into bite-sized pieces (see cook's note)

¼ teaspoon kosher salt

3 ounces soft goat cheese (chèvre)

12 sheets thawed phyllo dough

¼ cup melted ghee

1 Preheat the oven to 400°F. Preheat the salt block on the stove, beginning with low heat and gradually increasing the temperature to medium-high, until the surface temperature is 375°F to 400°F. Transfer the hot salt block to the middle rack in the oven.

2 Meanwhile, prepare the filling. In a nonstick skillet over medium heat, melt the butter. Add the mushrooms and salt, and sauté, stirring frequently, until the mushrooms release their liquid, about 5 minutes. Continue to cook until the liquid cooks off, 3 to 5 minutes more. Reduce the heat and stir in the goat cheese until melted. Set the filling aside while you prepare the phyllo dough.

3 To prepare the dough, unroll the package of phyllo and place a clean, barely damp dishtowel over it. Remove one piece of dough and place on a clean work surface, such as a pastry mat. Brush ghee over the entire piece of pastry. Place a second piece of dough over the buttered piece, and brush with butter. Continue until you have four layers of dough, each buttered, including the top piece. Use a pizza cutter or a pastry cutter to cut the rectangle in half crosswise to make two smaller pieces. Place a mound of filling (about 2 tablespoons) in the center of each piece, gather up the sides, and press together to seal. Continue repeating step three to make four more purses.

4 Remove the hot salt block from the oven, and place the six purses on the block. Return to the oven and bake at 400°F for 8 to 10 minutes, or until the dough is browned and crisp. Remove from the oven, and serve hot or warm.

COOK'S NOTE

Combine more exotic (and expensive) mushroom varieties with cremini mushrooms. You'll get the effect of wild mushrooms, but you'll pay a lot less. We use chanterelles, hen-of-the-woods, and maitake mushrooms as well as less expensive cremini mushrooms. Another way to get a deeper mushroom flavor is to drizzle the mushrooms with a little truffle oil or sprinkle them with truffle salt, after they've finished cooking.

WILTED MUSTARD GREENS WITH HONEY-ORANGE GLAZE

This is a gorgeous winter dish that is as visually pleasing as it is tasty. Note that the more moisture left on the mustard greens, the more salt imparted in cooking, so it is important for the greens to be as dry as possible.

SERVES 4

¼ cup honey

¼ cup sherry vinegar

2 tablespoons orange liqueur

2 bunches mustard greens

1 persimmon, cut into 16 wedges (peel if desired)

½ pomegranate, seeded

⅓ cup chopped toasted pecans

1　Preheat the salt block on the stovetop, beginning with low heat and gradually increasing the temperature to medium-high and then high, until the surface temperature is about 450°F.

2　Meanwhile, add the honey to a small saucepan. Cook over medium heat until the honey begins to darken, about 2 to 3 minutes. Use a pastry brush with water to touch up the sides of the pot to prevent the sugar from burning.

3　Add the sherry vinegar, bring to a boil, and reduce by half, about 5 minutes. Turn off the heat and add the orange liqueur. Return to a boil and reduce to a syrupy consistency that will coat a spoon, about 2 to 3 minutes. Remove from the heat and set aside.

4　Thoroughly wash and dry the mustard green leaves. Crush the thick rib of the stem to flatten or remove if desired.

5　Depending on the size of the mustard leaves, place one leaf at a time on the hot salt block until it begins to wilt, about 30 to 45 seconds. Then flip and cook the second side until wilted, about 15 to 20 seconds. Remove and set aside. Repeat for all of the leaves.

6　Chop the cooked mustard greens, and place in a medium serving bowl. Add the persimmon wedges, pomegranate seeds, and toasted pecans, and toss to combine. Drizzle the honey-orange glaze over the top and serve.

SALT-ENCRUSTED BAKED POTATOES

These baked potatoes have a creamy center with a nice aroma from the rosemary. Add your favorite toppings like sour cream and crispy bacon bits, but a simple pat of butter and freshly cracked black pepper is all these potatoes need. They also make a great base for your favorite twice-baked potato recipe.

SERVES 2 TO 4

2 large egg whites

2½ cups kosher salt

¼ cup chopped fresh rosemary (or any combination of herbs or spices you desire)

2 medium russet potatoes

1   Preheat the oven to 400°F. Preheat the salt block, beginning with low heat and gradually increasing the temperature to medium-high and then high, until the surface temperature is about 450°F.

2   In a small bowl, mix the egg whites, salt, and rosemary into a paste. Pierce each potato several times with the tines of a fork. Remove the hot salt block from the burner, and place the potatoes on the block. Using a large spoon and being very careful not to touch the salt block with you hands, completely encase each potato in the salt mixture.

3   Transfer the salt block to the middle rack in the preheated oven, and bake the potatoes for 1 hour. Remove from the oven. Break the salt crust and remove the potatoes, brushing off any excess salt. Cut in half, and serve with your favorite potato toppings.

SEARED ASPARAGUS WITH LEMON COMPOUND BUTTER

This recipe is deceptively simple: It has only four ingredients and takes mere minutes to make. It's a great recipe to try salt block cooking for the first time.

SERVES 4

2 tablespoons European-style butter, such as Plugrá, softened

1 teaspoon fresh lemon zest, from 1 lemon (reserve the lemon)

1 pound fresh asparagus

1 Preheat the salt block on the stove, beginning with low heat and gradually increasing the temperature to medium-high, until the surface temperature is around 375°F.

2 Meanwhile, make the compound butter. Place the butter in a small bowl, add the lemon zest, and stir to combine. Transfer the butter to a piece of plastic wrap and form into an oblong pat. Wrap and place in the refrigerator to chill.

3 Trim the stems from the asparagus (see cook's note). Wash the asparagus, and dry well with a paper towel or clean dishcloth.

4 Arrange the asparagus in a single layer on the hot salt block. Cook for 5 minutes, using tongs to occasionally roll the spears to cook evenly on all sides, until bright green, tender, and showing light sear marks.

5 Transfer the asparagus to four dinner plates. Unwrap the compound butter, cut into four slices, and place each piece on top of the hot asparagus so it melts. Cut the reserved lemon in half and squeeze about 1 to 2 teaspoons of juice over the asparagus. Serve immediately.

COOK'S NOTE

To determine where to trim an asparagus stem, bend the stem at the cut end with your hands. It will break naturally at the point where the most tender part of the asparagus ends. You can either trim all the asparagus this way or line up the asparagus on your cutting board and use a chef's knife to cut to the same length at once.

CUMIN-ROASTED CAULIFLOWER WITH GREEN CHILE CHIMICHURRI

We've put a Southwestern spin on cauliflower for this recipe, which makes a great side dish, but packs enough flavor to be served as an entrée.

SERVES 6

2 medium poblano peppers

1 cup roughly chopped Italian parsley leaves

½ cup roughly chopped cilantro leaves

¼ cup diced sweet onion

1 tablespoon diced jalapeño (optional)

½ teaspoon red pepper flakes

½ teaspoon kosher salt

2 cloves garlic

½ cup extra virgin olive oil plus 2 tablespoons, divided

2 tablespoons fresh orange juice

2 tablespoons red wine vinegar

1 large head cauliflower

2 teaspoons ground cumin

1   Preheat the oven to 450°F. Preheat the salt block, beginning with low heat and gradually increasing the temperature to medium-high and then high, until the surface temperature is about 550°F.

2   Meanwhile, cut the poblano peppers in half and remove the stems and seeds. Cut each half into four pieces that will lay flat. Lay the peppers skin side down on the hot salt block, and cook until the skin is mostly blistered, about 4 to 5 minutes. Remove and place in a plastic bag, seal, and let sit for 2 to 3 minutes to steam. Transfer the salt block to the middle rack of the oven. Remove the peppers from the bag, and peel off and discard the blistered skin.

3   Next make the chimichurri sauce. In the bowl of a food processor, add the poblano peppers and pulse about six to eight times, until the peppers are a large dice. Add the parsley, cilantro, onion, jalapeño, if using, red pepper flakes, salt, and garlic. Pulse until the mixture has a small dice consistency and is well combined, about ten pulses. Add ½ cup of the olive oil along with the orange juice and red wine vinegar, and process to combine, about 8 to 10 seconds. Set aside.

4   Remove the leaves from the cauliflower, slice the head in half, remove the core, and cut into florets. Add the florets to a large bowl, toss with the remaining 2 tablespoons of

olive oil, then sprinkle with the cumin to evenly coat. Spread evenly over the hot salt block and roast in the oven, stirring occasionally, until golden brown, about 20 minutes. Remove from the oven, and serve with the chimichurri sauce on the side.

COOK'S NOTE

We call for poblano peppers, as they are fairly mild and add a lot of flavor when roasted. The jalapeño adds a bite to the sauce, so eliminate it completely if you are sensitive to spice, or add more if you want to punch up the flavor. You will likely end up with leftover chimichurri sauce. To use the extra sauce, serve the cauliflower with Rib-Eye Steak (page 73)—the sauce goes particularly well with both dishes.

ROASTED BEET SALAD

Kelley loves no-waste recipes, and this one showcases how to use beets in their entirety. No more discarding the beet greens or carrot tops (see page 50 for how to make pesto from carrot tops).

SERVES 4

4 beets with greens, divided	2 teaspoons balsamic vinegar
1 orange	¼ cup extra virgin olive oil
1 teaspoon orange zest	kosher salt
1 teaspoon minced shallot	freshly cracked black pepper
1 teaspoon Dijon mustard	¼ cup toasted chopped walnuts
1 teaspoon honey	¼ cup soft goat cheese (chèvre)

1 Preheat the oven to 400°F. Preheat the salt block on the stove, beginning with low heat and gradually increasing the temperature to medium-high, until the surface temperature is about 400°F. Transfer the hot salt block to the middle rack in the oven.

2 Peel three of the beets, and cut each into 1-inch cubes. Lay them on the hot salt block and roast until tender, about 25 minutes, flipping with a metal spatula after 15 minutes.

3 While the beets are roasting, peel and grate the remaining beet into a medium bowl. Set aside. Wash the beet greens and pat dry. Remove the stems from the leaves and finely chop them, adding them to the grated beet. Chiffonade the greens by stacking the leaves on top of one another, rolling into a cigar shape, and beginning at one end, cutting into thin strips. Separate the strips, and toss with the grated beet and chopped stems. Set aside.

4 Zest half the orange and set aside. Cut off the top and bottom of the orange, just exposing the flesh. Place the fruit with one of the flat ends resting on your cutting board, and slice off the peel where the pith and flesh meet, following the curve of the side from top to bottom. Working over a small bowl to catch the juice, carefully cut along the membrane to free the segments. After removing all of the segments, squeeze the remaining juice from the peel and the membranes into the bowl. Set aside.

5 Add the orange zest, shallot, mustard, honey, and balsamic vinegar to the orange juice and whisk to combine. Add the olive oil in a steady stream, whisking constantly to emulsify the dressing. Season to taste with salt and pepper, and set aside.

6 Add the roasted beets, orange segments, and walnuts to the beet green mixture, and toss to combine. Add dressing as desired, and top with dollops of goat cheese. Serve.

COOK'S NOTE

If your beet greens are looking limp, refresh them in a bowl of ice water for about 15 minutes, and then pat them dry before cutting them into a chiffonade.

SEARED ROMAINE SALAD

You may never serve a raw green salad again after tasting salt-seared romaine lettuce. The romaine gets a bit of caramelization and picks up just the right amount of seasoning from the block. Add just a couple of ingredients and homemade dressing and you've got one flavorful salad.

SERVES 2

3 ounces white bread or 6 slices baguette, cut into 1-inch cubes (about 2 cups)

4 tablespoons extra virgin olive oil, divided

1 teaspoon minced shallot

1½ teaspoons honey

1 teaspoon Dijon mustard

½ teaspoon minced fresh thyme

1 tablespoon fresh lemon juice

1 head romaine lettuce

2 tablespoons grated Parmesan cheese

1   Preheat the oven to 375°F. Preheat the salt block on the stove, beginning with low heat and gradually increasing the temperature to medium-high, until the surface temperature is about 375°F. Transfer the hot salt block to the middle rack in the oven.

2   In a medium bowl, toss the bread cubes with 1 tablespoon of the olive oil. Spread the bread on the hot salt block and bake until golden brown, about 10 minutes. Set the croutons aside.

3   Transfer the salt block to the stove. Over medium-high heat, bring the surface temperature of the block to about 400°F.

4   In a small bowl, whisk together the shallot, honey, mustard, and thyme. Add the lemon juice, whisk to combine, and then slowly drizzle the remaining 3 tablespoons of olive oil into the mixture, whisking continuously to emulsify. Set aside.

5   Wash and dry the head of lettuce. Cut the lettuce in half lengthwise, keeping the core intact. Place the lettuce on the hot salt block cut side down, and cook until the lettuce shows a bit of browning, about 3 minutes. Note: Be careful not to overcook the lettuce as you want it to remain crisp.

6   To serve, lay each lettuce half on a plate and divide the croutons between the two plates. Drizzle the dressing evenly over the two halves, and sprinkle 1 tablespoon of grated Parmesan over each.

SALT AND VINEGAR
ROASTED POTATOES

This is a more sophisticated take on the popular salt and vinegar potato chip. The vinegar flavor is definitely present, but certainly does not have the puckering punch of the chip, making it a versatile side dish. These pair particularly well with pork chops or grilled sausage.

SERVES 4

4 medium red potatoes (about 1 pound)   1 cup white vinegar

4 cups water   2 teaspoons extra virgin olive oil

1   Preheat the oven to 400°F. Preheat the salt block on the stove, beginning with low heat and gradually increasing the temperature to medium-high and then high, until the surface temperature is about 450°F. Transfer the hot salt block to the middle rack in the oven.

2   Clean and cut the potatoes into ½-inch cubes.

3   Add the potatoes, water, and vinegar to a large pot, and bring to a boil over high heat. Boil for 1 minute. Turn off the heat, and let sit for 5 minutes, stirring after 2 minutes. Drain the potatoes in a colander, and shake off the excess water. Drizzle the olive oil over the potatoes, and toss to coat.

4   Spread the potatoes evenly over the hot salt block. Roast in the oven, turning the potatoes with a spatula after about 20 minutes for more even browning and salt seasoning. Roast until the potatoes are browned, about 40 minutes total.

BLISTERED GREEN BEANS WITH BACON VINAIGRETTE

Bacon and green beans is a classic combination, a pairing that's put to good use in this delicious side dish. On the hot salt block, the green beans sear until they blister. Toss them with bacon crumbles and a smoky, salty vinaigrette, and the result is perfection.

SERVES 4

2 slices thick-cut bacon

1 pound fresh green beans, ends trimmed

¼ cup red wine vinegar

1 Preheat the salt block on the stove, beginning with low heat and gradually increasing the temperature to medium-high, until the surface temperature is 375°F to 400°F.

2 Meanwhile, place the bacon in a large skillet and cook over medium-high heat, turning as needed, until the bacon is crisp, 8 to 10 minutes. Transfer the bacon to a paper towel. Leave about 2 tablespoons of bacon grease in the pan, and discard the rest.

3 Arrange the green beans in a single layer on the hot salt block (work in batches if they don't all fit). Let cook, turning occasionally with tongs, until the green beans are blistered and tender, 8 to 10 minutes. Turn off the head and transfer the cooked green beans to a bowl, and cover tightly with plastic wrap or aluminum foil as you cook the remaining beans.

4 When all the beans are cooked, warm the bacon fat in the pan over medium heat. Whisk in the red wine vinegar. Uncover the green beans and drizzle with the vinaigrette. Using a pair of tongs, toss the beans to coat evenly. Crumble the bacon over the beans.

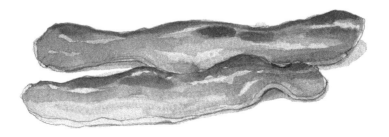

SEARED CARROTS WITH CARROT TOP PESTO

Pesto can be made using a lot of different types of herbs, nuts, and even cheeses. This version utilizes the green leafy carrot tops, which often get discarded. If your bunch of carrots aren't leafy enough, use parsley leaves to fill out the amount. Pecans can also easily replace the walnuts. You will likely end up with extra pesto and this isn't a bad thing! It is great in the morning on an egg sandwich, tossed with pasta, or on top of Baked Salmon (see page 95).

Sumac's bright, zesty flavor perfectly complements the sweetness of carrots. It may be found in the spice aisle of most specialty food stores. If you don't have sumac, sprinkle lemon zest or lemon zest and paprika over the carrots as a substitute.

SERVES 4

1½ cups roughly chopped carrot leaves

¼ cup chopped toasted walnuts

¼ cup shredded Parmesan cheese

1 large clove garlic, minced

¼ teaspoon lemon zest

2 teaspoons fresh lemon juice

⅓ cup plus 1 tablespoon extra virgin olive oil, divided

1 bunch (4–5) medium carrots

1½ teaspoons sumac

1 Preheat the salt block, beginning with low heat and gradually increasing the temperature to medium-high and then high, until the surface temperature is about 500°F.

2 Meanwhile, make the pesto. Place the carrot leaves, walnuts, Parmesan, garlic, and lemon zest in the bowl of a food processor. Pulse until coarsely chopped, about ten 1-second pulses. Add the lemon juice and ⅓ cup of olive oil, and process until incorporated, about 10 seconds. Set aside.

3 Peel the carrots, and coat with the remaining 1 tablespoon of olive oil. Sprinkle the sumac evenly over the carrots. Place the carrots on the hot salt block. Cook for 5 minutes, then turn and cook for 2 to 3 more minutes, until tender.

4 Serve the carrots on the block, or transfer the carrots to a serving platter, and top with pesto as desired.

SALT-ROASTED RADISHES

Raw radishes with butter and salt are a timeless culinary combination—and for good reason. Roasting the radishes adds a slight sweetness to their bite, making for a wonderful side dish.

SERVES 2

1 bunch radish with tops

2 tablespoons unsalted butter, room temperature

freshly cracked black pepper

1 Preheat the oven to 375°F.

2 Wash, dry, and mince the radish leaves. Put the knob of unsalted butter on a room temperature salt block, and add 2 tablespoons of radish leaves to the butter. Using an offset spatula, work the leaves into the butter, smearing the mixture across the salt block until incorporated. Reserve the butter and wipe the salt block clean.

3 Preheat the salt block on the stove, beginning with low heat and gradually increasing the temperature to medium-high, until the surface temperature is about 375°F. Transfer the hot salt block to the middle rack in the oven.

4 Trim the radish tops and bottoms. Cut each radish into quarters. Place on the hot salt block and roast for 15 minutes. Turn and roast until tender, about 5 additional minutes.

5 Once the radishes are done, transfer them to a serving bowl and toss with the butter. Finish with freshly cracked black pepper to taste.

PARSNIP-POTATO ROSETTES

We've given Duchesse potatoes a modern update with the addition of parsnips. We like the zip that they add to this classic, rich potato dish.

MAKES 18 TO 20

2 large russet potatoes

1 large parsnip

4 egg yolks, beaten

½ stick unsalted butter, room temperature

¼ teaspoon freshly cracked black pepper

⅛ teaspoon freshly grated nutmeg

1   Preheat the oven to 375°F. Preheat the salt block on the stove, beginning with low heat and gradually increasing the temperature to medium-high, until the surface temperature is about 375°F. Transfer the hot salt block to the middle rack in the oven.

2   Meanwhile, wash and peel the potatoes and parsnip. Cut into 1-inch cubes, add to a large saucepan, and cover with water by about 1½ to 2 inches. Bring to a boil over high heat, reduce the heat to medium-high, and simmer until tender, about 20 minutes. Turn off the heat. Set a colander in the sink, and drain the potatoes and parsnip.

3   Add the potatoes and parsnip back to the pot, and set over the warm burner. Mash with a potato masher until smooth, allowing steam to evaporate. Remove from the burner, and let cool for a few minutes before adding the egg yolks and butter. Fold in until completely incorporated. Season with the black pepper and nutmeg.

4   Add the mixture to a large pastry bag with a star tip. Pipe the mixture into rosettes about 2 inches in diameter and 2 inches tall on the hot salt block.

5   Return the salt block to the oven and bake the rosettes until golden brown, about 15 to 20 minutes.

BROCCOLI RABE WITH RED PEPPER FLAKES, LEMON ZEST, AND PARMESAN

Broccoli rabe, also referred to as rapini, is a sophisticated cousin to broccoli. It's deep green flavor and nice bitter bite complement everything from Baked Salmon (see page 95) to Rib-Eye Steak (see page 73).

SERVES 4

1 Meyer lemon

1 bunch broccoli rabe

2 tablespoons extra virgin olive oil

½ teaspoon red pepper flakes

2 tablespoons shredded Parmesan cheese

freshly cracked black pepper

1   Preheat the salt block, on the stove, beginning with low heat and gradually increasing the temperature to medium-high and then high, until the surface temperature is about 500°F.

2   Zest the Meyer lemon and set aside. Cut the lemon in half, saving half for a later use.

3   Coat the broccoli rabe in the olive oil, and place on the hot salt block. Cook for 5 minutes. Place the lemon half flesh side down on the salt block then turn the broccoli rabe and cook for 2 to 3 more minutes, until tender.

4   To serve, plate the broccoli rabe and sprinkle the reserved lemon zest, red pepper flakes, and Parmesan cheese over the top. Squeeze the lemon juice on top, and season with a few turns of freshly cracked black pepper.

COOK'S NOTE

It is best to use smaller stems of broccoli rabe for this recipe. If you get thicker stems, cut them in half lengthwise or opt to finish them in a 400°F oven until tender so they do not get oversalted. Depending on the size of the broccoli rabe, you might need to cook them in batches or on two salt blocks if they don't all fit on one block without overcrowding.

ROASTED BRUSSELS SPROUTS WITH APPLE CIDER REDUCTION

We love the way tangy-sweet apple cider is the perfect foil for the earthy, barely bitter flavor of brussels sprouts. And when you reduce it long enough, it thickens into a lovely, glazelike sauce. Depending on the size of the brussels sprouts, you might need to cook them on two salt blocks if they don't all fit (since they take nearly 30 minutes to cook, preparing them in batches, as in other faster-cooking recipes probably isn't feasible).

SERVES 4

1 pound brussels sprouts

1 tablespoon extra virgin olive oil

1 cup apple cider

¼ cup apple cider vinegar

1 Preheat the oven to 400°F. Preheat the salt block on the stove, beginning with low heat and gradually increasing the temperature to medium-high, until the surface temperature is 375°F to 400°F. Transfer the hot salt block to the middle rack in the oven.

2 Meanwhile, prepare the brussels sprouts. Trim a sliver off each stem, and halve each sprout from stem to end. Discard any leaves that fall off. Place in a bowl, drizzle with the olive oil, and toss to coat.

3 Remove the hot salt block from the oven, and arrange the sprouts on the block, cut side up. They can be close together, even touching, but they should be in a single layer. Return the sprouts to the oven, and cook for 25 to 30 minutes, or until slightly wilted and browned.

4 While the sprouts are cooking, combine the apple cider and apple cider vinegar in a small saucepan, and simmer over medium heat until syrupy and reduced by about two-thirds. Remove from the heat and let cool slightly in the pan. When the sprouts are done, transfer them to a serving bowl, and drizzle the cider reduction over them. Serve hot.

Brussels sprouts give off a lot of liquid when they cook, so be sure that all of the sprouts are cut side up when you arrange them on the block. Otherwise they'll become too salty.

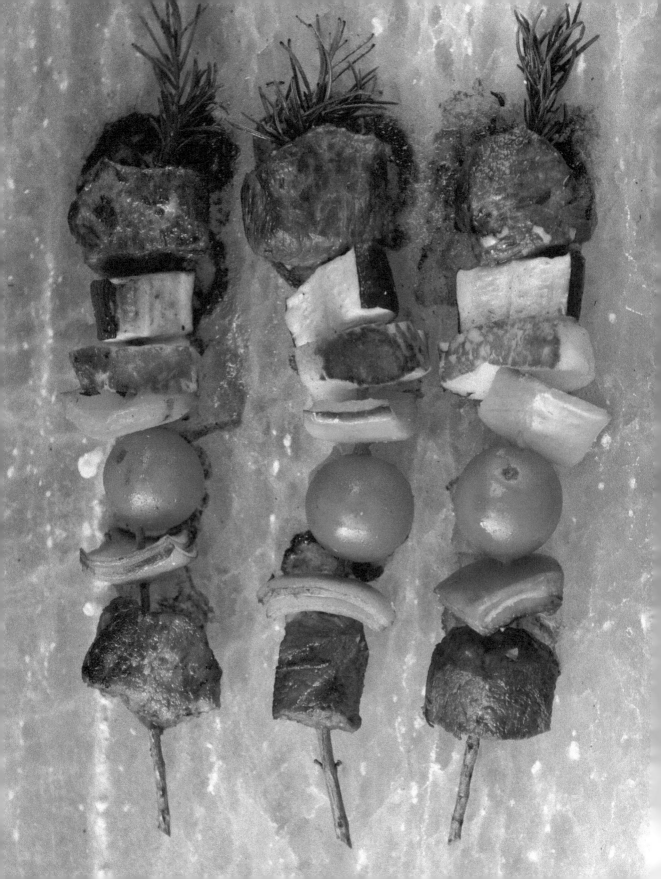

CHAPTER 3

MEAT, FOWL, AND EGG

Cooked on a salt block, meat develops a perfect crust on the exterior while retaining its juices inside. The salt absorbed from the block gives the meat just the right amount of seasoning. And just as a little sprinkling of salt is the perfect addition to a rich egg, we discovered that preparing eggs with the salt block is a wonderful–and unexpected–technique.

SALT-SIZZLED CHICKEN TACOS

Use this flavorful chicken as a taco or burrito filling (use the corn tortillas on page 103), topped with lettuce, pico de gallo, avocado, cotija cheese, or your favorite taco fixings. It's also excellent sliced atop taco salad, or on a Southwestern-flavored club sandwich. For a smoky variation, substitute chipotle powder for the red chili powder.

SERVES 4

1 teaspoon ground cumin
¼ teaspoon garlic powder
¼ teaspoon red chili powder

1 pound boneless, skinless chicken breast pieces
corn tortillas
grated cheese, lettuce, tomatoes and other taco fixings

1 Heat the salt block on the stove, beginning with low heat and gradually increasing the temperature to medium-high and then high, until the surface temperature is around 450°F.

2 Meanwhile, stir together the cumin, garlic powder, and chili powder in a small bowl, and set aside. Place the chicken between two pieces of parchment paper or plastic wrap, and use a meat mallet to pound to an even thickness of about ½ inch. Rub both sides of the chicken with the spice mixture, repeat with the remaining chicken.

3 Place the chicken on the hot salt block (work in batches if there isn't enough room). Cook for 8 to 10 minutes, until browned, then turn and cook for 8 to 10 minutes more, until cooked through. The meat should be 165°F when checked internally with a meat thermometer.

4 Remove from the salt block, let rest a few minutes, and slice into strips on the diagonal with a knife. Serve in corn tortillas with the toppings of your choice.

COOK'S NOTE

If you don't have a meat mallet, you can use the bottom of a wide glass jar or the bottom of a heavy pan to pound the chicken. Use leftover chicken by finely dicing it and mixing it with mayonnaise, pickled jalapeños, and diced red bell pepper for a Southwestern chicken salad.

CHICKEN SATAY

Serve this satay at a party or alongside rice and stir-fried vegetables for dinner. Sambal oelek is a fresh ground chile paste found in most Asian grocery stores and adds a hint of heat to the peanut sauce.

MAKES ABOUT 12 STRIPS

For the Chicken

½ cup coconut milk

2-inch piece of lemongrass, cut in half

1-inch piece of peeled ginger, cut in half

1 clove garlic

zest of ½ lime

¼ teaspoon red pepper flakes

1 pound boneless skinless chicken breast

For the Peanut Sauce

½ cup creamy peanut butter

¼ cup coconut milk

1 tablespoon soy sauce

1 teaspoon fresh lime juice

2 teaspoons sambal oelek

2 tablespoons warm water

1 Place the coconut milk, lemongrass, ginger, garlic, lime zest, and red pepper flakes in a blender, and puree until smooth. Slice the chicken breast into ½-inch-wide strips, and place in a medium bowl. Pour the coconut milk mixture over the top, and toss to completely coat the chicken. Cover with plastic wrap, and refrigerate for at least 2 hours.

2 Preheat a salt block on the stove or grill, beginning with low heat and gradually increasing the temperature to medium-high and then high, until the surface temperature is about 550°F.

3 To make the peanut sauce, place the peanut butter, coconut milk, soy sauce, lime juice, and sambal oelek in the blender, and puree until smooth, about 45 seconds. Add the warm water and blend until combined, about 15 seconds. Set aside.

4 Remove the chicken slices from the marinade, and thread on small, wooden skewers (one slice per skewer), and lay them on the hot salt block. Cook until the edges turn opaque and the bottom is browned, about 3½ minutes. Flip and cook until the second side has browned and the chicken is cooked through to 165°F, about 3½ minutes. To serve, place three skewers on each of four plates and divide the peanut sauce evenly among four small serving bowls.

COOK'S NOTE

Don't bother rinsing the blender between making the coconut milk marinade and the peanut sauce. Any residue from the marinade will simply add to the flavor of the peanut sauce.

CHICKEN WITH LEMON, CAPERS, AND PARSLEY

This simple recipe is quick and refreshing, perfect for a weeknight dinner. It really showcases how effectively a salt block can sear meat and give it a lovely, seasoned crust. We suggest serving this chicken with a simple, classic side dish like rice pilaf, buttered pasta, or mashed potatoes.

SERVES 4

4 small (4-ounce) boneless, skinless chicken breast pieces

freshly ground black pepper

1 lemon, halved

1 tablespoon minced fresh Italian parsley

2 tablespoons capers

1   Preheat the salt block on the stove, beginning with low heat and gradually increasing the temperature to medium-high, until the surface temperature is around 400°F.

2   Meanwhile, prepare the chicken. Place a breast between two pieces of plastic wrap and use a meat mallet to pound it to a uniform thickness of about ½ to ¾ inch. Repeat with the remaining chicken breasts.

3   Lightly pepper both sides of each breast, and arrange on the hot salt block (work in two batches if all the breasts don't fit). Cook for about 7 to 9 minutes on the first side, until browned, then flip and cook around 5 to 7 minutes on the other side, until browned and cooked through when checked with a knife. Keep cooked breasts warm under aluminum foil until all are cooked.

4   Place the chicken on plates or a platter, squeeze lemon over the top, and sprinkle on the parsley and capers. Serve immediately.

COOK'S NOTE

If you prefer a less briny taste, you can rinse the capers in a small colander or sieve before using.

SALT-CURED EGG YOLKS

Humble egg yolks transform into a savory seasoning when cured with salt. Patience is a necessity, as these yolks will take several weeks to cure. We don't know where the recipe originated, but the equal ratio of salt to sugar is pretty standard and adapts well for the salt block. Be very gentle with the yolks as they break easily (discard any that do). Grate a cured egg yolk over salad, pasta, asparagus, or Beef Carpaccio (see page 32).

MAKES 12 CURED YOLKS

1 cup kosher salt

1 cup granulated sugar

1 dozen egg yolks

1 Chill a salt block in the refrigerator for several hours or overnight.

2 In a shallow bowl, stir together the salt and sugar; reserve ½ cup. Working carefully to keep the yolk intact, add one egg yolk to the salt and sugar mixture. Lightly coat, then transfer the yolk to the salt block. Repeat for all 12 egg yolks. Cover with cheesecloth and place the block on a sheet pan. Refrigerate for 5 days.

3 Remove from the refrigerator and add one egg yolk to the reserved salt and sugar mixture. Lightly coat, then transfer to the salt block with the side that had previously been on the salt block now exposed to air. Repeat for all 12 egg yolks. Cover with cheesecloth and place the block on a sheet pan. Refrigerate for 5 more days.

4 Remove from the refrigerator, and brush off any excess salt. Place the yolks directly on a cooling rack to expose the yolks to air on all sides and cover with cheesecloth. Refrigerate for another 2 to 3 weeks until dry. Store eggs up to 1 month in a cool, dry place.

VEAL AND HARICOTS VERTS BUNDLES WITH LEMON SAUCE

These bundles are a bright combination of flavors and make an elegant presentation for dinner, whether you are entertaining guests or serving a romantic dinner. For a variation of this recipe, you could substitute chicken or pork cutlets for the veal.

MAKES 4

For the Sauce

3 tablespoons unsalted butter, divided

1 tablespoon minced shallot

½ teaspoon minced garlic

¼ cup white wine

1 teaspoon Dijon mustard

1 cup chicken stock

2 tablespoons fresh lemon juice

½ teaspoon lemon zest

1 tablespoon finely chopped Italian parsley

kosher salt

freshly cracked black pepper

For the Veal and Haricots Verts Bundles

4 veal scaloppine (2–2½ ounces each)

freshly cracked black pepper

½ pound haricots verts, stem ends trimmed

1 teaspoon grapeseed oil

1 Preheat a salt block on the stove or grill, beginning with low heat and gradually increasing the temperature to medium-high, until the surface temperature is about 400°F.

2 Meanwhile, make the sauce. Melt 1 tablespoon of the butter in a medium saucepan over medium-high heat. Add the shallot and sauté until translucent, about 2 minutes. Add the garlic and cook, stirring constantly, about 30 seconds. Add the white wine, bring to a boil, and reduce by half, 3 to 4 minutes. Whisk in the mustard. Add the chicken stock, bring to a boil, and reduce by two-thirds, 7 to 9 minutes. Whisk in the lemon juice, and cook for another minute. Turn off the heat, and whisk in the remaining 2 tablespoons of butter. Stir in the lemon zest and parsley, and lightly season to taste with salt and pepper. Cover to hold.

3 Place the veal between two pieces of plastic wrap or wax paper. Using a meat mallet, gently pound out the veal until ⅛ inch thick. Season with cracked black pepper.

4 Coat the haricots verts in the grapeseed oil. Spread them evenly over the hot salt block. Cook, turning occasionally, until bright green and showing some searing, about 3 minutes. Remove and set aside.

5 Lay two pieces of veal on the salt block. Cook until the edges begin to curl and are browned on one side, about 2 to 2½ minutes. Turn and cook the second side until browned, about 2 minutes. Remove from the salt block, keep warm. Repeat with the remaining two pieces of veal.

6 Evenly divide the haricots verts into four bundles. Place a bundle at the end of each scaloppine, and roll the veal, secure with a toothpick or decorative cocktail pick. Pour the sauce over the top, and serve.

RABBIT ROULADES STUFFED WITH CHERRIES AND PECANS

While in culinary school, Jessica made rabbit roulades for her boyfriend for a special Valentine's Day dinner. Her ambition paid off — they've been married over 10 years now! If you are not intimidated by cutting up a whole chicken, you won't have any trouble cutting up a rabbit as their bone structure is surprisingly similar. You can find great visual instructions or videos online, or you can ask your butcher to cut up and debone the rabbit for you.

SERVES 4

1 tablespoon extra virgin olive oil

¼ cup chopped leeks

¼ cup chopped toasted pecans

¼ cup chopped dried cherries

½ cup finely ground cornmeal

1 teaspoon plus more kosher salt, divided

¼ teaspoon plus more freshly ground black pepper, divided

1 whole rabbit, about 4 pounds, skinned, innards removed

1   With the oven rack in the middle position, preheat the oven to 375°F. Preheat the salt block on the stove, beginning with low heat and gradually increasing the temperature to medium-high, until the surface temperature is 350°F to 375°F.

2   Meanwhile, prepare the filling. In a small skillet, heat the olive oil over medium heat. Add the leeks and sauté, stirring frequently, until translucent and soft. Stir in the pecans and cherries, and season lightly with salt, to taste. Remove from the heat, and set aside. In a shallow dish, such as a pie pan or a breading tray, combine the cornmeal with 1 teaspoon salt and ¼ teaspoon black pepper.

3   To prepare the rabbit, place it on its back. With a very sharp boning knife, cut the flap of skin along the ribcage toward the spine, cutting underneath the loin piece near the spine to keep it attached to the flap of skin. You should end up with the entire loin and a flap of skin attached. Repeat with the other loin. Cut away the hind legs from the torso, then make a cut to the bone along the length of the legs and use a paring knife or the tip of the butcher knife to carefully remove the bone from the leg, resulting in a boneless piece of meat, similar to a chicken thigh. The remaining pieces of rabbit can be used for stock. Season the insides of all the cut pieces with salt and pepper.

4   Spoon about 1 tablespoon of the leek filling mixture onto the center of the thin skin attached to the loin and use clean hands to spread it out a bit (be careful not to let the

spoon come in contact with the raw meat so you can use the remaining stuffing as a garnish). Starting with the loin, roll it tightly around the filling. Secure with butcher twine on either end and at least once in the middle to keep the bundles intact. Repeat with the other loin piece, and with the two leg pieces. Pat the bundles dry with a paper towel.

5 Roll the bundles in the cornmeal mixture, then arrange on the hot salt block on the stove. Sear for 2 minutes on each side, then transfer the rabbit and salt block to the preheated oven and cook for 15 to 20 minutes, or until the internal temperature is 160°F when checked with a meat thermometer.

6 Let rest for 5 minutes, then cut each piece into slices on the diagonal. Sprinkle the remaining pecan-cherry mixture over the top before serving.

SALT-FRIED EGG IN THE HOLE

A childhood favorite, egg in the hole is a fun variation on the basic fried egg. This recipe works best if your salt block is relatively new, with a surface that is still very smooth so that the egg has less chance of sticking.

SERVES 1

1 teaspoon ghee, divided, or as needed   1 egg
1 slice sandwich bread

1 Preheat the salt block on the stove, beginning with low heat and gradually increasing the temperature to medium-high, until the surface temperature is around 375°F.

2 When the salt block is hot, spread about ½ teaspoon of ghee over the hottest part of the block, in an area just slightly larger than the size of your bread. Place the bread on top of the melted ghee, and let toast for about 2 minutes or until lightly browned.

3 Using a round metal biscuit cutter about 2 inches in diameter, cut a circle in the center of the bread (you can do this directly on the block or remove the bread to a cutting board first). Flip the bread over on the salt block so the toasted side is up, place another ½ teaspoon of ghee in the middle and when it melts, crack the egg in the hole. Cook for 4 to 6 minutes, until the egg white is completely cooked through. Place the circle cutout on the block, toasted side up. If desired, flip over the entire egg and toast combination after the white and yolk have set, and cook 1 to 2 minutes on the other side. Remove from the salt block and serve immediately, with the round cutout also on the plate to sop up extra egg yolk.

SOUTHERN QUENCHER PORK CHOPS

One of Kelley's favorite chicken recipes, a Sweet Tea-Brined Chicken from *Southern Living*, inspired this recipe. Plan ahead as you will want to allow the marinade enough time to chill before adding the pork chops. The key to getting good color on the chops without the sugars burning is to turn the chops at regular intervals as instructed.

SERVES 4

4 cups water

6 black tea bags, such as Lipton

½ cup fresh lemon juice

1 cup sugar

4 (1½-inch-thick) bone-in pork chops

freshly cracked black pepper

1 In a large saucepan over high heat, bring the water to a boil. Turn the heat to low, and add the tea bags. Brew the tea until dark, about 6 to 8 minutes. Take out the tea bags, squeezing out any excess liquid. Remove from the heat, add the lemon juice and sugar, and stir constantly until the sugar is completely dissolved, about 1 to 2 minutes. Allow the liquid to cool completely, then refrigerate until cold.

2 Place the pork chops in a large freezer bag and pour in the marinade. Refrigerate for at least 12 hours and up to 24 hours.

3 Preheat the salt block on the grill according to the instructions on page 7, until the surface temperature is about 550°F.

4 Remove the pork chops, and pat dry with paper towel. Lightly season both sides with black pepper. Place two chops on the salt block and cook for about 8 minutes, turning every minute until browned on both sides. Continue to cook 4 to 6 additional minutes, flipping after 2 to 3 minutes, until done. Remove from the salt block and keep warm. Repeat with the remaining two pork chops.

COOK'S NOTE

You can cool the tea quickly by filling your sink with ice water deep enough to set the saucepan in so that the ice water comes up the sides of the pot without spilling over into the pot. Stir the liquid until cool, then refrigerate until cold.

SEARED BEEF WITH NAPA CABBAGE

You could substitute flank steak or flat iron steak if skirt steak is not available at your grocery store.

SERVES 2-4

For the Marinated Beef

¼ cup fresh orange juice

1 tablespoon sambal oelek

2 teaspoons minced fresh ginger

2 cloves garlic, minced

½ teaspoon orange zest

½ teaspoon fish sauce

1 pound skirt steak

For the Dressing

2 tablespoons fresh orange juice

1 teaspoon tamari

½ teaspoon Dijon mustard

½ teaspoon orange zest

2 tablespoons peanut oil

For the Cabbage

1 orange

1 medium napa cabbage

2 tablespoons chopped cilantro

2 tablespoons minced fresh mint

2 tablespoons chopped peanuts

1 To make the marinade, whisk together the orange juice, sambal oelek, ginger, garlic, orange zest, and fish sauce in an 8-inch square baking dish. Add the skirt steak and coat on all sides with the marinade, cover with plastic wrap, and refrigerate for a minimum of 2 hours, turning the meat after 1 hour.

2 Preheat a salt block on the stove, beginning with low heat and gradually increasing the temperature to medium-high, until the surface temperature is about 400°F.

3 Meanwhile, prepare the orange for the beef. Cut the top and bottom off the orange, just exposing the flesh. Set one of the flat ends on your cutting board, and slice off the peel where the pith and flesh meet, following the curve of the side from top to bottom. Working over a small bowl to catch the juice, carefully cut along the membrane to free the segments. After all of the segments have been removed, squeeze the remaining juice from the peel and the membranes. Reserve the fresh juice for the dressing.

4   To make the dressing whisk together the orange juice, tamari, mustard, and orange zest in a small bowl. Slowly add the peanut oil, whisking continuously to combine. Set aside.

5   Cut the cabbage into quarters and remove the core. Place the cabbage on the hot salt block cut side down, and cook until a bit of browning shows, about 3 minutes. Turn the cabbage to the other cut side, and cook until it begins to brown, between 2 and 3 minutes. Note: Be careful not to overcook the cabbage, as you want it to remain crisp.

6   Turn the heat to high and let the block's temperature rise to 550°F to cook the steak.

7   Lay the steak on the hot salt block, and cook for 3 minutes. Flip and cook for another 3 minutes. Flip again and continue to cook until browned, about 2 to 3 minutes. Then flip and cook until the second side has browned and the meat is cooked. Remove from the salt block, cover with foil, and rest for 2 to 3 minutes.

8   Slice the beef into ½-inch-wide strips, cutting against the grain of the meat. Add the meat and orange segments to a medium bowl and toss to combine. Chop the cabbage wedges in half and toss the wedges in the dressing. For a dramatic presentation, fan out the cabbage wedges on a plate and serve the beef and orange mixture on the side. Top the beef with the cilantro, mint, and peanuts.

RIB-EYE STEAK

Kelley's father-in-law likes a nicely seared outer crust on his steak, so for this one, she really turned up the heat on the salt block. Top with a savory compound butter and this will be your go-to preparation for sizzling rib-eye.

SERVES 2

2 rib-eye steaks, 1½ inch thick
freshly cracked black pepper

savory compound butter (page 111)

1 Preheat a salt block on the grill according to the instructions on page 7, until the surface temperature is about 550°F to 600°F.

2 Season both sides of each steak with pepper, as desired. Place the steaks on the hot salt block and cook for 5 minutes, until a nice brown crust forms.

3 Turn the steaks, and cook until a crust forms on the second side and the steak has reached desired doneness, 4 to 5 minutes for medium-rare.

4 Top each steak with 1 slice of savory compound butter, and serve.

COOK'S NOTE

We recommend preparing steaks on a grill because of potential flare-ups from fat dripping off the block if you have a gas stovetop.

KOREAN-STYLE SHORT RIBS

A sticky, sweet-and-tangy sauce is the trademark of Korean short ribs. Ordinarily, the meat is coated in the sauce before cooking, but we found that doing so on the salt block turns the sauce into a tarry black mess. Instead, season the ribs and grill them, then slather them with sauce before serving.

SERVES 4

4 cloves garlic, minced, divided

4 teaspoons grated fresh ginger, divided

1½ pounds short ribs, flanken style or boneless and thinly sliced

⅓ cup brown sugar

⅓ cup soy sauce

½ teaspoon sesame oil

freshly ground black pepper

4 cups cooked brown or white rice

8 to 12 large lettuce leaves, such as romaine

¼ cup fresh cilantro

1   Preheat the salt block on the stove, beginning with low heat and gradually increasing the temperature to medium-high, until the surface temperature is 375°F to 400°F.

2   Meanwhile, combine two cloves of the garlic and 3 teaspoons of the ginger, and lightly rub the mixture on the short ribs. Set aside.

3   To make the sauce, combine the remaining two cloves of garlic and 1 teaspoon of ginger along with the brown sugar, soy sauce, sesame oil, and black pepper as desired in a small saucepan. Bring to a simmer and cook, stirring frequently, until the sugar dissolves and the mixture thickens slightly, 3 to 4 minutes. Set aside.

4   When the salt block is hot, arrange the short ribs on the block, working in batches if they all don't fit. Cook for 4 to 6 minutes on one side, or until browned, then turn and cook for another 4 to 6 minutes on the other side. Remove from the block, and place on a serving platter. Keep the cooked ribs warm under aluminum foil until all the meat has cooked. Drizzle the meat with about half of the sauce, reserving the other half to add more to the lettuce wraps as needed. Serve with cooked rice, big lettuce leaves to wrap, and cilantro to garnish.

Beef short ribs are available three ways: English style, in which the meat is separated along the bone; boneless, which comes in a thick chunk; and flanken style, in which the meat is thinly sliced across the bone. For this recipe, choose either flanken style or boneless ribs that have been thinly sliced.

CUBAN SANDWICH

The Cuban sandwich from Puerto Sagua restaurant in Miami Beach, Florida was the inspiration for turning two hot salt blocks into a panini press. Be very careful when handling the hot salt blocks, and use protective oven mitts.

MAKES 1 SANDWICH

1 Cuban roll or 6-inch soft baguette
unsalted butter, room temperature
1 teaspoon yellow mustard
1 slice Swiss cheese

2 ounces honey-baked ham, finely sliced
2 ounces roasted pork, sliced
3 slices dill pickle

1 Preheat two salt blocks on the stove, beginning with low heat and gradually increasing the temperature to medium-high, until the surface temperature is about 350°F to 375°F.

2 Meanwhile, flatten the roll with the palm of your hand. Slice the roll in half, and lightly spread the butter on the outside of the bread. Spread the mustard on the inside of each half. Place the cheese and then the ham on the bottom half of the roll, and lay the pork on the top half.

3 Lay both halves meat side up on one of the hot salt blocks. Using protective oven mitts, carefully lay the second hot salt block on top of the meat, with the cooking side down. Cook for 30 to 45 seconds, then remove the top block. Lay the pickle slices over the ham, and top with the pork half of the sandwich. Carefully replace the second hot salt block on top of the sandwich and press down on the top salt block; cook for 3 to 3½ minutes. Remove the top block, cut the sandwich in half on the diagonal, and serve warm.

COOK'S NOTE

You could substitute sliced bread for the roll, Dijon mustard for the yellow, turkey for the roasted pork, provolone for the Swiss cheese. Not a fan of pickles? Leave them out. Like mayonnaise? Add it! Use this recipe more as a guide to making your own delectable creations. If you choose not to heat the meat in step 3, heat the blocks to about 350°F and add extra press time for your sandwich to heat through.

LAMB CHOPS WITH SPICED MUSTARD CRUST

Juicy, rich lamb chops are a lovely treat for a special dinner. We use rib chops (see cook's note) for this recipe because they make such a stunning presentation, but you can use loin chops, which are a little more economical. A word of warning: Because lamb is fatty, a lot of fat will drip off the meat onto your block, so be prepared to do some scrubbing (see our recommendations for cleaning in the introduction). We suggest preparing this recipe on an older, more seasoned salt block.

SERVES 4

1 tablespoon extra virgin olive oil

2 teaspoons Dijon mustard

2 cloves garlic, minced

½ teaspoon ground ginger

½ teaspoon ground coriander

¼ teaspoon ground turmeric

¼ teaspoon kosher salt

8 (2– to 3–ounce) lamb rib chops, trimmed of excess fat

¾ cup fine breadcrumbs

½ teaspoon garlic powder

1 Preheat the salt block on the stove, beginning with low heat and gradually increasing the temperature to medium-high, until the surface temperature is 375°F to 400°F.

2 Meanwhile, combine the olive oil, mustard, garlic, ginger, coriander, turmeric, and salt in a small bowl. Brush both sides of each chop with the mixture, place on a plate or in a shallow dish, and let rest for 20 minutes. In another shallow dish, combine the breadcrumbs and garlic powder.

3 When the salt block is hot, dredge each chop in the breadcrumb mixture and place on the hot block. Cook for 4 to 5 minutes on each side, until the chops are cooked through but still very pink on the inside, or to the desired doneness. Serve immediately.

COOK'S NOTE

This recipe uses rib chops, which are the chops along the base of the ribcage. The meat is very tender, moist, and flavorful. You can buy a rack of lamb and cut them apart yourself between the ribs, or you might have a butcher who sells the individual rib chops. Look for a rack or chops that are already frenched, which means that the meat and tissue have already been cleaned from the bone.

LAMB AND HALLOUMI KEBABS

These kebabs are packed with flavor and will likely become a regular part of your dinner rotation. Serve with couscous on the side and substitute yellow summer squash for the halloumi cheese if desired.

MAKES 12 KEBABS

12 rosemary sprigs

6 (3–ounce) lamb loin chops

¼ cup plus 2 tablespoons extra virgin olive oil, divided

zest of 1 lemon

2 tablespoons fresh lemon juice

2 tablespoons minced fresh mint

1 tablespoon minced fresh rosemary

2 cloves garlic, minced

6 ounces halloumi cheese

1 small zucchini

½ large red bell pepper, cored and seeded

½ red onion

12 cherry tomatoes

1   Remove all but the top leaves from the rosemary sprigs. These will be your skewers. Cut the meat off the bone, trim the fat, and cut into approximately 1½-inch pieces. In a medium bowl, combine ¼ cup of the olive oil and the lemon zest, lemon juice, mint, rosemary, and garlic. Add the lamb and toss to coat with the marinade, cover with plastic wrap, and refrigerate for at least 2 hours.

2   Preheat a salt block on the grill according to the instructions on page 7, until the surface temperature is about 550°F.

3   Cut the halloumi into 1¼-inch cubes. Coat them with the remaining 2 tablespoons of olive oil. Cut the zucchini in half lengthwise and then into 1-inch-thick half moons. Cut the bell pepper and red onion into 1-inch chunks.

4   Beginning with lamb meat, thread the kebab. Add one zucchini moon, one piece of halloumi, one pepper, cherry tomato, and one onion, followed by another piece of lamb.

5   Place three skewers on the hot salt block, and cook until the meat is browned, about 4 minutes. Flip the skewer, and cook the other side until the meat is browned and cooked to medium, about 4 minutes. Place on a serving platter, and keep warm under aluminum foil as you cook the remaining skewers.

COOK'S NOTE

Halloumi cheese has a high melting temperature, making it good for grilling and is often sold in 8-ounce packages. Grill the remaining cheese and any leftover vegetables that do not fit on the skewers to serve on the side or as leftovers for lunch.

CHAPTER 4

SEAFOOD MAINS

Succulent seafood lends itself well to a beautiful presentation on a chilled salt block or to cooking on a hot salt block. The hot, griddlelike surface cooks the seafood quickly, sealing in the delicate flavor and moisture. If you try no other recipe in this chapter, give the Whole Snapper in Salt Crust (page 83) a try—it's a stunning preparation that yields a moist, super-flavorful result.

SIZZLING PEEL-AND-EAT SHRIMP

This fun recipe is meant for a casual night in. Eat the shrimp as fast as you can pull it off the salt block—and don't worry about messy, greasy fingers because that's part of the fun! The larger the shrimp, the more expensive they are, but bigger shrimp are definitely better for this recipe as they'll stay juicy and offer more reward for the work of peeling them. So buy the biggest shrimp you can afford. Frozen is just fine, but thaw the shrimp before cooking it.

SERVES 4

½ stick unsalted butter

2 cloves garlic, minced

2 pounds large shrimp, shells on, deveined (see cook's note)

¼ cup minced fresh Italian parsley

1 Preheat the salt block on the stove, beginning with low heat and gradually increasing the temperature to medium-high, until the surface temperature is 375°F to 400°F.

2 Meanwhile, melt the butter in a small saucepan and stir in the garlic. Turn off the burner, cover, and keep warm.

3 Arrange the shrimp in a single layer on the hot salt block (work in batches if needed, and keep the uncooked shrimp on ice). Cook for 3 minutes, turning halfway through cooking, until the shrimp are pink, opaque, and curled. Transfer the cooked shrimp to a serving bowl, drizzle with the butter and garlic mixture, and sprinkle on the parsley.

COOK'S NOTE

To devein shrimp while leaving the shell on, use a paring knife or kitchen shears to cut through the shrimp shell along the length of the back, cutting a little into the flesh of the shrimp. Use the tip of the knife to pull out the dark, stringy vein.

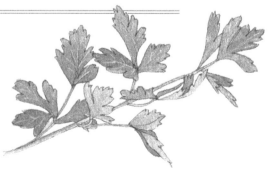

WHOLE SNAPPER IN SALT CRUST

For a dramatic presentation, you can't beat this whole fish baked in a salt crust. At the table, the crust is cracked open with a hammer or a meat mallet and pulled away to reveal fish that's possibly the most tender and succulent you've ever had. When you buy a whole fish, ask the fishmonger to clean the inside and descale the fish, but to leave the skin on. It helps keep the fish moist.

SERVES 4

1 whole snapper, cleaned and descaled (2½ to 3 pounds)

1 lemon, cut into quarters, plus an additional lemon cut into wedges for serving

5 sprigs thyme

9 to 10 cups (3 pounds) coarse kosher or sea salt

3 egg whites

½ cup water, or more if needed

1 Preheat the oven to 400°F. Preheat the salt block on the stove, beginning with low heat and gradually increasing the temperature to medium-high, until the surface temperature is 375°F to 400°F.

2 Meanwhile, prepare the fish by rinsing inside and out and patting dry. Stuff the cavity with the quartered lemon and the thyme, wrap loosely in plastic, and refrigerate.

3 In a large bowl, mix the salt, egg whites, and ½ cup water or more, if needed, until the mixture clumps together when a handful is squeezed.

4 Set the hot salt block on a rimmed baking sheet. Place the fish on the block, and working quickly, pack the salt mixture over the entire fish, covering it completely in a thick layer and pressing lightly on the salt to compress it so it holds together. Place in the oven, and cook for 20 minutes. Check for doneness by pushing the probe of an instant-read thermometer through the salt crust until it reaches the fish. When the thermometer registers 145°F, remove the fish from the oven.

5 To serve, crack the crust with a hammer or meat mallet and pull chunks of it away from the fish. Peel off the skin, then use a fork or a knife to pull the meat off the ribcage in large pieces, arranging them on a serving tray or on dinner plates. Turn the fish over, remove the skin, and pull the meat off the other side. Serve immediately with lemon wedges.

SALMON AVOCADO SUSHI

Want to impress the guests at your next party? A pristine pink salt block is a lovely receptacle on which to display handmade sushi. Making basic sushi rolls (called maki in Japanese) is really quite simple, and these days "exotic" ingredients like rice vinegar, wasabi (Japanese horseradish), pickled ginger, and sheets of nori (dried seaweed) are easy to find at a well-stocked supermarket or at an Asian market, if you are lucky enough to have one nearby. Otherwise, buy these ingredients online; Marukai eStore (www.marukaiestore.com) is a reasonably priced source. The only specialty tool you will need to make the sushi is a bamboo rolling mat, which is inexpensive and can be found at Asian grocery stores and specialty cookware stores. If you can't find one, use a clean woven dishtowel instead.

MAKES 4 SUSHI ROLLS, CUT INTO 6 PIECES EACH

For the Sushi Rice

1½ cups sushi rice (2 standard rice cooker cups)

1⅞ cups water, or amount needed per your rice cooker's instructions

2 tablespoons rice vinegar

1 tablespoon granulated sugar

1 teaspoon sea salt

For the Sushi

4 sheets nori

wasabi, as needed

½ pound wild Alaska salmon fillet, pin bones and skin removed, cut into thin strips

1 avocado, thinly sliced into strips

1 tablespoon white sesame seeds, or a combination of black and white sesame seeds

soy sauce, pickled ginger, wasabi for serving

1 Chill a salt block in the refrigerator for a few hours.

2 If using a rice cooker, rinse the rice in the insert, rubbing handfuls between your fingers, until the water is no longer cloudy. Drain, and add the water for cooking the rice as per your rice cooker's instructions. Set the rice cooker to the "regular" or "sushi rice" setting. After the rice is done (cooking times will vary according to model), let it sit, covered, for 10 minutes.

If cooking on the stovetop, rinse the rice in a strainer. Bring the cooking water to a boil, add the drained rice, and lower the heat to a simmer. Cook, covered, for 15 minutes or until the rice is tender and the water is mostly absorbed. Remove from the heat and let stand, covered, for 10 minutes.

3 While the rice is cooking, combine the rice vinegar, sugar, and salt in a small glass dish. Microwave for 30 seconds until hot and the sugar and salt granules are dissolved. Drizzle the vinegar mixture over the cooked rice, and use a flat spatula or a wooden spoon to mix it well into the rice. This process should cool the rice and separate any lumps.

4 To make the sushi, lay a sheet of nori, shiny side down, on the rolling mat or dishtowel. Nori has lines that can be used as a cutting guide. Make sure that the lines are perpendicular to you. Spread the cooled rice on the nori, only a few grains of rice thick, over the entire sheet. Use the back of the spoon to spread a very thin layer of wasabi lengthwise about ½ inch from the edge of the nori closest to you. Arrange slices of salmon and avocado over the wasabi.

5 Starting with the edge of the nori closest to you, tightly roll the nori inside the mat, pulling the mat back a bit from the rolled part as the sushi rolls onto itself. When the nori is completely rolled but still covered with the mat, squeeze it inside the mat to compress it and even out the roll. Remove the mat and slice the sushi along the guidelines into 6 pieces. Repeat with the remaining sushi.

6 Arrange the sushi pieces, cut side down, on the chilled salt block. Sprinkle the sesame seeds as a garnish. Serve with soy sauce, pickled ginger, and wasabi.

SALT-KISSED SCALLOPS ON ARUGULA WITH TARRAGON VINAIGRETTE

Scallops work beautifully oven-cooked on a salt block. Their tender flesh picks up just enough salt flavor, and the spicy greens and tangy vinaigrette round out the flavors of this dish.

SERVES 4

¼ cup tarragon vinegar

½ teaspoon Dijon mustard

kosher salt

¼ cup extra virgin olive oil

freshly ground black pepper

1 pound sea scallops (about 16 to 20)

6 ounces baby arugula (about 4 cups, loosely packed)

1   With the oven rack in the middle position, preheat the oven to 400°F. Preheat the salt block on the stove, beginning with low heat and gradually increasing the temperature to medium-high, until the surface temperature is 375°F to 400°F. Transfer the salt block to the oven.

2   Meanwhile, make the vinaigrette. In a medium bowl, whisk together the vinegar, mustard, and a pinch of salt until smooth. Gradually drizzle in the olive oil, whisking continuously, until the mixture emulsifies. Season to taste with additional salt as needed and black pepper. Set aside.

3   Pat the scallops dry with a paper towel. Remove the salt block from the oven, arrange the scallops on the salt block, and return it to the oven. They should sizzle when they make contact with the block. Cook 3 minutes, then use tongs to turn the scallops over and cook an additional 3 minutes. The scallops are done when they are lightly browned and opaque.

4   While the scallops are cooking, place the arugula in a large bowl, and drizzle with the vinaigrette (whisk to re-emulsify if the vinaigrette has separated). Use tongs or salad servers to toss the greens to coat evenly with the vinaigrette.

5   Place about 1 cup of salad on each plate. Divide the scallops evenly among the plates, arranging them on top of the greens.

CRAB CAKES

Crab cakes are simple to make, especially if you purchase pre-picked crab meat. Our version is light and bright and is good for breakfast with poached eggs and hollandaise, for lunch with a fresh green salad, and as an appetizer for dinner.

MAKES 6

12 saltine crackers (about ½ cup crumbs)

1 pound picked crab meat

¼ cup grated sweet onion

2 tablespoons minced fresh Italian parsley

2 teaspoons Old Bay seasoning

1 teaspoon lemon zest

½ teaspoon red pepper flakes

1 large egg, beaten

2 tablespoons fresh lemon juice

grapeseed oil

1   Place the saltines in the bowl of a food processor, and process into fine crumbs, about 10 to 15 seconds.

2   In a large bowl, mix together the crab meat and grated onion. Add the saltine crumbs, parsley, Old Bay seasoning, lemon zest, and red pepper flakes, and mix to combine. Add the egg and lemon juice, mix to combine, cover with plastic wrap, and refrigerate until the salt block is nearly heated.

3   Preheat the salt block on the grill, beginning with low heat and gradually increasing the temperature to medium-high, until the surface temperature is about 400°F.

4   Remove the crab mixture from the refrigerator. Using a ½ cup measure, portion out the crab and form into patties. Brush the hot salt block generously with grapeseed oil, and place the crab cakes on the block. Cook until the bottom has crisped and browned, about 8 to 10 minutes. Using a metal spatula, carefully flip each crab cake. Cook the second side until browned and cooked through, approximately 8 to 10 minutes. Serve warm.

COOK'S NOTE

We don't specify a type of crab for this recipe since it works equally well with varieties available from both coasts.

BLOCK CURED SALMON

Making your own cured salmon, similar to lox or gravlax, is surprisingly easy—really all you need is weight and time. A salt block makes the ideal weight, and you can even use the larger pieces of a broken block. For the best texture, make sure to use fresh, top-quality salmon fillets, and preferably salmon that hasn't been frozen. We like wild Pacific coho or sockeye.

MAKES ABOUT ¾ POUND CURED SALMON

½ cup coarse kosher salt

¼ cup granulated sugar

1 teaspoon finely grated lemon zest
(about 1 lemon)

1 teaspoon dried dill

1 pound fresh salmon, skin on, descaled
and pin bones removed

1 In a bowl, combine the salt, sugar, lemon zest, and dill. Spread a handful of the salt mixture over a salt block. With the remaining salt mixture, coat both sides of the salmon, pressing it into the fish.

2 Place the salmon skin side down on the salt block, and top with additional salt mixture if there's any left. Place another salt block on top of the fish. Set a cooling rack or a trivet in a baking sheet, and transfer the salt blocks with the fish between them to the rack or trivet to keep it slightly elevated. Cover the whole thing loosely with plastic wrap, and refrigerate for 24 to 48 hours, until the salmon is pressed thin and is dense and compacted.

3 Rinse the cured salmon well and pat dry. To serve, cut very thin slices horizontally. The fish will keep, wrapped in plastic and refrigerated, for 3 to 4 days.

TUNA AND PINEAPPLE SKEWERS

Use the best possible quality tuna for this easy recipe, which is delicious served over brown rice or on a green salad. While the recipe calls for using the stovetop, cooking on the grill is also a good option.

SERVES 4 (2 TO 3 SKEWERS EACH)

1 whole pineapple

1 pound fresh tuna (preferably sushi-grade ahi), cut into 1-inch chunks

¼ cup rice vinegar

2 teaspoons soy sauce

½ teaspoon sesame oil

1 teaspoon grated or minced fresh ginger

1 Preheat the salt block on the stove, beginning with low heat and gradually increasing the temperature to medium-high, until the surface temperature is 375°F to 400°F. If opting for the grill, preheat the salt block according to the instructions on page 7, until the surface temperature is about 400°F.

2 Meanwhile, prepare the pineapple. Using a chef's knife, slice off the top and the bottom. Set the pineapple upright on a cutting board, and slice the rind off in strips, from top to bottom. Turn the pineapple on its side and cut in half lengthwise, then cut each half into four wedges. Cut off the core that is the point of each wedge, and cut the wedges into 1-inch chunks.

3 Beginning and ending with a piece of pineapple, alternate chunks of pineapple and tuna on long skewers. In a small bowl, combine the vinegar, soy sauce, sesame oil, and ginger. Brush the mixture onto the skewered tuna and pineapple, making sure to coat all sides.

4 Place the skewers on the hot salt block, working in batches if they don't all fit. Cook for 2 to 3 minutes, until the exterior is seared, then flip and cook 2 to 3 minutes on the other side. Serve immediately.

SALT-SUGAR CURED SHRIMP WITH KIMCHI RICE

This recipe requires a chilled salt block and a separate block for cooking. The sugar on the shrimp caramelizes as it cooks, playing nicely off the spicy kimchi rice. A demo by Andrew Zimmern at the South Beach Food and Wine Festival inspired the rice, and Kelley adapted a technique for crispy skillet rice she learned from Chef Linton Hopkins of Restaurant Eugene to great effect.

SERVES 2 TO 4

1 pound medium shrimp, peeled and deveined

¼ cup granulated sugar

1½ cups cooked white rice

1 cup chopped kimchi

2 scallions, cut on the bias, divided

2 tablespoons kimchi juice

¼ teaspoon sesame oil

1 Chill a salt block in the refrigerator for several hours or overnight.

2 Preheat the second salt block on the stove, beginning with low heat and gradually increasing the temperature to medium-high and then high, until the surface temperature is about 500°F.

3 Place the shrimp and sugar in a medium bowl, and toss to coat the shrimp. Lay the shrimp on the chilled salt block and refrigerate for 15 to 20 minutes, depending on the size of the shrimp.

4 In a large bowl, combine the rice, kimchi, whites of the scallions, kimchi juice, and sesame oil, and stir to combine. Set aside.

5 Arrange the shrimp on the hot salt block, and cook until they are opaque halfway up the side, about 1½ to 2 minutes. Flip and cook until done, approximately 1½ minutes. Remove from the salt block, and set aside in a serving bowl.

6 Spread the kimchi rice mixture on the hot salt block, and cook until the bottom of the rice begins to crisp, about 4 to 5 minutes. Using a metal spatula, flip the rice and cook for 2 to 3 more minutes until completely heated through. Add the kimchi rice to the shrimp, and toss to combine. Top with the remaining scallions, and serve.

SHRIMP SLIDERS

Sliders make for a playfully pleasing presentation. Go beyond the burger with these shrimp sliders. While small in size, they are big on flavor!

MAKES 8 TO 10

For the Sriracha Mayo

1 egg yolk, room temperature

2 teaspoons fresh lemon juice

1 tablespoon Dijon mustard

¾ cup canola oil

½ teaspoon sriracha

For the Pickled Red Onion

¼ cup rice vinegar

½ teaspoon sugar

⅛ teaspoon kosher salt

1 teaspoon minced jalapeño (optional)

½ red onion, finely sliced

For the Sliders

1 pound shrimp, peeled and deveined

¼ cup panko

1 tablespoon minced cilantro

¼ teaspoon minced fresh ginger

1 egg, beaten

2 tablespoons tamari or soy sauce

1 teaspoon fresh lime juice

¼ teaspoon wasabi paste (optional)

canola oil

1 package slider buns

butter lettuce leaves

½ cucumber, sliced

1   Make the sriracha mayo. In a medium bowl, whisk the egg yolk. Add the lemon juice and mustard, and whisk to combine. Slowly add the oil, whisking continuously, until incorporated. Continue whisking until the mayonnaise thickens. Reserve all but ¼ cup for later use. The mayonnaise will keep for up to 1 week in the refrigerator. Add the sriracha to the ¼ cup mayonnaise, and whisk to combine. Set aside in the refrigerator.

2   Make the pickled red onion. Add the vinegar, sugar, and salt to a small bowl, and whisk to dissolve. Stir in the minced jalapeño, if using, and set aside. Bring a large pot of water to a boil. Add the red onion slices, blanch for 2 minutes, and drain in a colander. Add the onion to the vinegar mixture, toss to coat, and then submerge in the liquid. Cover with plastic wrap, and set aside.

3   Place the shrimp in the bowl of a food processor, and pulse to chop into a large dice, about five to seven pulses. Add the panko, cilantro, and ginger, and pulse to combine, about five to seven pulses.

4   In a small bowl, whisk together the egg, tamari, lime juice, and wasabi paste if using. Add to the shrimp mixture, and pulse to combine, about five to seven pulses. Transfer the mixture to a medium bowl, cover with plastic wrap, and refrigerate for about 30 minutes.

5   Meanwhile, preheat a salt block on the grill according to the instructions on page 7, until the surface temperature is about 450°F.

6   Using a ¼ cup measure, portion out the shrimp and form into slider patties. Brush the hot salt block generously with canola oil, and place the sliders on the block. Cook until the bottom has crisped and browned, and the patty has turned opaque about halfway up the side, about 6 to 7 minutes. Using a metal spatula, carefully flip each slider. Cook the second side until browned and cooked through, approximately 5 to 6 minutes.

7   To serve, cut the buns in half and place on the grill to warm, then spread sriracha mayonnaise on the top side. Place one slider patty on the bottom half of each roll, and top with one lettuce leaf, two or three cucumber slices, pickled onions, and the top half of the bun.

COOK'S NOTE

Hawaiian rolls may be substituted for slider buns and add a slightly sweet contrast to the sriracha mayonnaise.

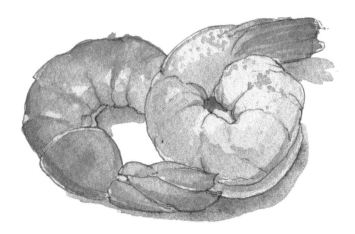

BAKED SALMON

This salmon is incredibly simple to make, demonstrating how cooking on a salt block is great for every day meals. This is a delectable way to prepare salmon and is a dramatic presentation, especially when served with the leftover carrot top pesto from page 50.

SERVES 2 TO 4

1 pound salmon fillet, pin bones removed

grapeseed oil

kosher salt

freshly crack black pepper

1 Preheat the oven to 375°F. Preheat the salt block on the stove, beginning with low heat and gradually increasing the temperature to medium-high, until the surface temperature is about 375°F.

2 Brush the block with grapeseed oil. Season the flesh of the salmon with salt and pepper as desired. Lay the salmon skin side down on the hot salt block. Place in the oven and bake 5 to 6 minutes for medium-rare, 7 to 8 minutes for medium, and 9 to 10 minutes for opaque throughout.

COOK'S NOTE

It's best to select a portion of salmon fillet that is as even as possible and fits on one salt block.

CHAPTER 5

BREADS ON THE BLOCK

A salt block can function much in the same way as a pizza stone, creating a hot cooking surface that beautifully crisps up a crust. Or it can be used as a griddle to brown softer doughs and batters. For wetter doughs and batters, make sure to prep the hot salt block with a little ghee or vegetable oil before using it, so your baked goods won't stick.

CHEWY BAGEL BITES

Making bagels is a fun project, perfect for a weekend afternoon. Pick your favorite toppings and make a few of each version. Be sure that you choose instant yeast and not active dry yeast, which needs to be activated in water before using.

MAKES 24 TO 32, DEPENDING ON SIZE

1 package instant yeast

3 cups unbleached bread flour, or more as needed

1½ teaspoons kosher salt

2 teaspoons brown sugar

9 ounces very warm water (around 120°F)

canola or vegetable oil, for oiling the bowl

For Water Bath and Cooking

1 tablespoon baking soda

1 tablespoon brown sugar

1 egg white

1 tablespoon water

2 tablespoons melted ghee

toppings (see cook's note)

1 In the bowl of a stand mixer, combine the yeast, flour, salt, and sugar. Use a whisk to combine and break up any lumps of brown sugar. Fit the stand mixer with a dough hook, add the warm water, and mix on low speed until a dough forms, adding more flour if it seems too sticky. Run the mixer on medium-low for 10 minutes to knead. Transfer the dough to a lightly oiled bowl, cover with a clean cloth, and let rise for 1 hour in a warm place.

2 After 1 hour, transfer the dough to a lightly floured work surface, divide into four pieces, and roll each into a long snake. Cut into 1-inch pieces. Cover loosely with plastic wrap, and let rise for 30 more minutes until puffy.

3 Meanwhile, preheat the oven to 425°F. Preheat the salt block on the stove, beginning with low heat and gradually increasing the temperature to medium-high and then high, until the surface temperature is 400°F to 425°F.

4 Fill a large pot with water, add the baking soda and sugar, and bring to a boil. In a small bowl, whisk the egg white with about 1 tablespoon of water, and set aside.

5 When the water is boiling, drop the bagel bites into the pot, a few at a time. Let cook for 1 minute, flip with a slotted spoon, and boil for 1 minute on the other side. Transfer to a baking sheet and boil the remaining bagel bites.

6 Brush the bagels lightly with the egg white mixture, and sprinkle with the desired toppings. Brush the salt block with the ghee to minimize sticking, and arrange the bagel bites on top. Transfer to the oven and bake for 15 to 18 minutes, or until golden but still soft when pressed. Remove from the oven, and transfer the bagel bites to a cooling rack.

COOK'S NOTE

Bagel bites can have a variety of toppings. Here are some of our favorites:

- Melted butter and granulated garlic
- Sesame seeds
- Poppy seeds
- Rosemary and sea salt
- Finely grated Asiago cheese

FLATBREAD, TWO WAYS

Once you try a flatbread or pizza baked on a salt block, you might never go back to cooking on a regular baking sheet or even a pizza stone again! This recipe will give you crisp crusts, with just the tiniest hint of salt seasoning to accentuate the bold-flavored toppings. We give you two different versions for the toppings; you can do either or both since the recipe yields several flatbreads. The ingredients listed for the flatbreads below will top roughly two flatbreads each, so double the ingredients if you are making only one type. Cut into small wedges, these flatbreads make a great party snack.

MAKES 4 FLATBREADS, EACH ABOUT 12 BY 8 INCHES

1¼ cups very warm water (about 115°F to 120°F)

1 tablespoon active dry yeast

1 tablespoon honey

3 cups all-purpose flour, divided, plus more for dusting

½ teaspoon salt

canola oil, for oiling the bowl

For Mediterranean Flatbread

2 tablespoons extra virgin olive oil

½ cup pitted and halved or roughly chopped kalamata olives

½ cup sliced roasted red peppers

1 cup baby arugula

⅓ cup crumbled feta cheese (about 2 ounces)

For Flatbread with Bitter Greens, Serrano Ham, and Fresh Mozzarella

2 tablespoons extra virgin olive oil

1 cup mustard greens chiffonade

1 ounce Serrano ham, cut into strips

3 ounces fresh mozzarella, cut into chunks, or mini mozzarella balls, halved

1   Pour the water into a large mixing bowl, then sprinkle the yeast over the water. Stir in the honey and 1 cup of the flour. Let rest for 20 minutes to activate the yeast; the mixture should be bubbly. With a wooden spoon, stir in the salt and the remaining 2 cups of flour until a shaggy dough forms. Turn the dough out onto a lightly floured work surface, and knead to form a smooth, elastic dough. Continue kneading for 5 minutes to strengthen the glutens in the dough, then form into a smooth ball. Wash the mixing bowl, coat the interior lightly with canola oil, and place the dough in the bowl, turning the dough over to coat it. Cover with a clean dishtowel, and let rise for 30 to 45 minutes, until salt block is heated.

2 With the oven rack in the middle position, preheat the oven to 450°F. Preheat the salt block on the stove, beginning with low heat and gradually increasing the temperature to medium-high and then to high, until the surface temperature is 425°F to 450°F. Transfer to the hot oven.

3 When the salt block is hot, cut the dough in four equal pieces. Cover the remaining pieces while you work with one piece. Roll or pat one piece of dough into a rough rectangle, about the dimensions of your salt block. Remove the hot salt block from the oven. Using a pizza peel or folding the dough over your arm, quickly and carefully transfer the dough to the hot block, immediately adjusting it if needed to cover the surface without hanging off the sides.

4 Now you're ready to make either the Mediterranean flatbread or the flatbread with bitter greens, Serrano ham, and fresh mozzarella. For both flatbreads, brush the dough lightly with olive oil, and return to the oven, baking for 5 minutes, or until the dough is dry to the touch.

5 Remove from the oven, and spread half the ingredients for either type of flatbread, in the order listed, evenly over the bread. Return to the oven, and cook for 5 minutes more, or until the ingredients are hot and the cheese is soft. Remove the salt block from the oven. Transfer the flatbread to a cutting board. Repeat with the remaining flatbreads and ingredients. After cooking and transferring to a cutting board, let the flatbread sit for 3 to 4 minutes, and then use a pizza cutter to cut into wedges or slices. Serve hot or warm.

COOK'S NOTE

Since this recipe requires the salt block to be moved in and out of a very hot oven, a salt block holder and silicone mitts are essential. If you don't have them, try putting your salt block on a baking sheet to make it easier to get it in and out of the oven.

CORN TORTILLAS

With only three ingredients and a few minutes of time, you can make fresh, tender corn tortillas, which have a much better flavor and texture than their store-bought counterparts. Using a salt block on the stove as a griddle replicates the hot griddle or cast iron surface that is the traditional method of cooking these Mexican breads.

Masa harina, the finely ground corn flour made from dried corn soaked in limewater, can be found in the international section of most supermarkets, or at a Mexican grocery store.

MAKES 8 TORTILLAS

1 cup masa harina, plus more for dusting

¼ teaspoon kosher salt

¾–1 cup lukewarm water

1 Heat the salt block on the stove, beginning with low heat and gradually increasing the temperature to medium-high, until the surface temperature is 350°F to 375°F.

2 Meanwhile, combine the masa and salt in a mixing bowl. With a fork, stir in enough water to make a clumpy, moist dough. Gather the dough and give a couple of kneads, just enough to form a ball. Place the ball on a work surface sprinkled lightly with additional masa. Flatten the ball slightly into a disk, and cut into eight wedges with a bench scraper or a knife. Keep the pieces of dough under plastic wrap to avoid drying out.

3 Work with one piece of dough at a time. Roll the dough into a ball, flatten it slightly on the work surface, and then form the tortilla. Either use a tortilla press or roll the dough into a thin circle, about 5 to 6 inches in diameter, with a rolling pin.

4 Cook the tortilla on the hot salt block for 45 seconds to 1 minute, until the underside is dry and brown spots begin to form. Flip it over with a metal spatula, and cook for 1 to 1½ minutes more on the other side. Keep cooked tortillas warm under a clean towel while you cook the remaining dough.

COOK'S NOTE

For a simple snack, fill the fresh tortillas with slices of queso fresco cheese, a slice of avocado, and some roughly chopped cilantro. Or use the tortillas with Salt-Sizzled Chicken Tacos (page 59).

SALT-COOKED DINNER ROLLS

Soft, yeasty rolls get deliciously crisp on the bottom when baked on a hot salt block. This recipe requires two rises, so be sure to plan accordingly. It's well worth the wait. Make sure that you choose instant yeast and not active dry yeast, which needs to be activated in water before using.

MAKES 12 ROLLS

½ cup whole milk

3 tablespoons unsalted butter, divided

2 cups all-purpose flour, divided, plus more for dusting

2 tablespoons sugar

½ teaspoon salt

1½ teaspoons instant dry yeast

1 egg yolk

1 teaspoon flaky sea salt

1 In a small saucepan, heat the milk and 2 tablespoons of the butter until the mixture is about 120°F to 130°F. In a stand mixer fitted with a dough hook, combine 1 cup of the flour and the sugar, salt, and yeast. On the lowest speed, add the milk mixture and the egg yolk. Beat until a sticky dough forms. With the mixer on low, gradually add the remaining 1 cup of flour until the dough forms a ball. Run the mixer on low speed for about 5 minutes to knead the dough.

2 Turn the dough out onto a lightly floured surface, pat into a disk, and divide into 12 pieces with a bench scraper or a knife. Form each piece into a ball, cover the balls loosely with plastic wrap, and let rise about 30 minutes.

3 Meanwhile, preheat the oven to 375°F with the oven rack in the middle position. Preheat the salt block on the stove, beginning with low heat and gradually increasing the temperature to medium-high, until the surface temperature is 350°F to 375°F.

4 When the oven and salt block are hot, melt the remaining 1 tablespoon of butter in the microwave or on the stove. Arrange the rolls on the salt block, brush the tops with the melted butter, and sprinkle on the sea salt. Place in the oven and bake for 12 to 15 minutes, or until the rolls are lightly browned. Remove from the salt block to a cooling rack. Serve warm or at room temperature.

If you don't have a stand mixer, you can make these rolls by hand. Combine the ingredients in a mixing bowl with a wooden spoon, then turn the mixture out onto a floured work surface and knead for 5 minutes.

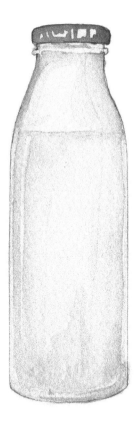

GARLICKY SOFT FLATBREAD

One of our favorite treats when we go out for Indian food is the pile of pillowy, piping-hot naan that the waiters bring to the table for scooping up every drop of the delicious curries. We've developed this version, a cross between a pita and naan, especially to make on a hot salt block. Brushed with garlic-infused ghee, it's just the thing to serve with lentil stew, a spicy curry, or a Middle Eastern dip like hummus or baba ghannoush. Or try it with Edamame "Hummus" (page 30).

MAKES 12 FLATBREADS, ROUGHLY 5–6 INCHES IN DIAMETER

1 package (2½ teaspoons) instant yeast

1 teaspoon granulated sugar

⅔ cup warm water (about 120°F)

½ cup warm milk (about 120°F)

1½ cups all-purpose flour, plus more for dusting

1½ cups whole wheat flour

1 teaspoon kosher salt

4 teaspoons extra virgin olive oil, plus more for coating the bowl

¼ cup ghee

2 cloves garlic, minced

1 In the bowl of a stand mixer fitted with the dough hook, combine the yeast, sugar, water, milk, all-purpose flour, whole wheat flour, salt, and 4 teaspoons olive oil. Begin mixing at low speed, gradually increasing the speed as the ingredients come together into a soft dough. When all the ingredients are combined, mix at medium speed for 5 minutes to knead the dough.

2 Lightly coat the inside of a clean mixing bowl with olive oil, and remove the dough from the stand mixer, form into a ball and place inside the oiled mixing bowl. Turn over to coat the dough with the oil, cover loosely with a clean dishtowel or plastic wrap, and let rise in a warm place for 45 minutes to an hour. The dough should almost double in size.

3 Preheat the salt block on the stove, beginning with low heat and gradually increasing the temperature to medium-high, until the surface temperature is 350°F. Place the ghee and garlic in a small saucepan or metal bowl, and set it on the salt block to melt, removing when melted.

4 Meanwhile, turn the dough out onto a lightly floured work surface and use a bench scraper or a knife to divide it into 12 equal pieces. Roll each piece into a ball, then cover with plastic wrap. Working with one ball at a time and keeping the others covered, roll into a circle, about 5 or 6 inches in diameter.

5 When the salt block is heated, remove the ghee if you haven't done so already, and place the pan near the stove on a trivet. Put two rounds of dough on the salt block, and cook for 3 minutes, or until the underside is browned. Flip the bread over, brush the top with the garlic ghee, and cook for 1 to 2 minutes more. Repeat with the remaining dough, keeping the cooked flatbreads stacked on a plate under aluminum foil to keep warm. Serve warm or at room temperature.

SCALLION PANCAKES

Scallion pancakes are a Chinese dish typically cooked in a skillet with a generous amount of oil. The salt block version uses less oil and still gets nice browning on the pancake.

MAKES 8 PANCAKES

2½ cups all-purpose flour, plus more for dusting

1 cup water

3 tablespoons plus 1⅛ teaspoons sesame oil, divided

½ cup soy sauce

2 teaspoons sambal oelek

2 bunches scallions

canola oil

1 Place the flour in the bowl of a food processor. Bring the water to a boil, and add 1 tablespoon of the sesame oil to the boiling water. While the food processor is running, slowly add the water containing the oil through the feed tube, and process until a ball forms. Turn the dough out onto a lightly floured work surface, and scrape out any dough that sticks to the sides to the bowl. Knead the dough for about 5 minutes until smooth, adding more flour to your work surface as needed to prevent sticking. Then knead the dough on a room-temperature salt block for about 30 seconds to season. Coat the ball of dough with 1 teaspoon of the sesame oil, wrap in plastic, and let rest at room temperature.

2 Preheat the salt block on the stove, beginning with low heat and gradually increasing the temperature to medium-high and then high, until the surface temperature is about 550°F. Preheat the oven to 200°F.

3 Meanwhile, make the dipping sauce by whisking together the soy sauce, sambal oelek, and ⅛ teaspoon of the sesame oil in a small bowl. Set aside.

4 Spread one bunch of scallions on the hot salt block, and cook for 3 minutes, or until the onions begin to wilt. Turn and cook for 2 more minutes, or until roasted and showing lightly charred spots. Remove from the heat, let cool, and repeat with the second bunch. Cut off the root end of the onions and chop.

5 On a lightly floured work surface, roll the dough to about ¼ inch thick. Brush with the remaining 2 tablespoons of the sesame oil, and spread the onions out evenly over the surface. Beginning on the long side, roll the dough into a log, then roll the log into a coil like a cinnamon roll. Press into a disk and evenly cut into eighths.

6 Roll each eighth of dough into a ball, then flatten each ball into a disk. Roll each into a circle about ¼ inch thick. Brush both sides of each pancake with canola or some other neutral cooking oil. Place one pancake in the center of the salt block, and cook for 3 minutes, until golden brown. Flip the pancake, and cook for 2 to 3 minutes. Transfer to a pie plate, and place in the oven to keep warm. Repeat with the remaining pancakes. Cut each pancake into quarters, and serve warm with the dipping sauce.

COOK'S NOTE

You can skip the step of cooking the scallions and simply use chopped, raw scallions if preferred. You can also add picked crab, cooked shrimp, crushed Sichuan peppercorns, or other ingredients to create your own variation as desired.

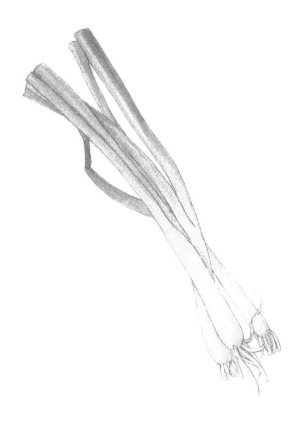

SOUTHERN DROP BISCUITS

Steaming buttermilk biscuits smothered in sorghum or honey butter are a Southern delight. While not absolutely necessary, chilling your bowl and all of the ingredients before assembling this recipe will make for fluffier biscuits.

MAKES 10 TO 12 BISCUITS

2 cups all-purpose flour

1 tablespoon baking powder

1 tablespoon sugar

1 stick unsalted butter, frozen

1 cup buttermilk

canola oil for greasing

1 Preheat the oven to 350°F. Preheat the salt block on the stove, beginning with low heat and gradually increasing the temperature to medium-high, until the surface temperature is about 350°F. Transfer the salt block to the middle rack in the oven.

2 In a medium bowl, whisk together the flour, baking powder, and sugar.

3 Shred the frozen butter on a chilled box grater, and add to the dry ingredients. Toss with a fork to combine, making certain the shredded butter does not clump together. Add the buttermilk, and stir until the dough is just combined.

4 Grease a ¼ cup measuring cup with canola oil, and use it to portion the dough. Place the portioned dough on the heated salt block.

5 Bake for about 20 to 25 minutes, until the biscuits are golden brown. Remove from the oven and transfer to a wire baking rack. Allow to cool for a few minutes before serving.

6 Repeat with the remaining dough.

COOK'S NOTE

To make sorghum or honey butter, simply combine 1 stick of unsalted butter at room temperature with ¼ cup sorghum or honey. Of course, we recommend spreading this onto a chilled salt block and letting it rest for about a minute in order to add a little salt.

COMPOUND BUTTERS

A compound butter is simply butter that's been mixed with a flavoring agent, whether sweet or savory. It's a versatile condiment that can be used on grilled steak, slathered on hot yeast rolls, or tossed with steamed vegetables. A chilled salt block makes a good surface for mixing the butter with its flavorings, and the butter will pick up a hint of the complex Himalayan salt flavor. Use our flavoring suggestions to start with, and you'll soon be coming up with your own flavors and combinations!

You can use high-quality, fresh store-bought butter, or you can make your own with heavy cream and a stand mixer. Either way, make sure that the butter is very soft but not melty when you work with it.

MAKES 4 OUNCES

1 stick butter, such as Plugrá, very soft

Sweet Flavoring Options (choose one)

1 tablespoon local honey

½ teaspoon cinnamon

1 teaspoon cocoa powder plus 1 teaspoon powdered sugar

1 tablespoon maple syrup

Savory Flavoring Options (choose one)

1 tablespoon minced fresh tarragon

1 teaspoon lemon zest plus ½ teaspoon lemon juice

1 teaspoon minced fresh thyme

1 teaspoon blue cheese

½ teaspoon minced rosemary

1 tablespoon minced fresh dill

1 tablespoon grainy mustard

1 tablespoon minced shallot

1 tablespoon minced cilantro plus 1 teaspoon lime

1 Chill a salt block in the refrigerator for several hours or overnight.

2 Place the butter on the chilled salt block. Using a wooden or stiff rubber or plastic spatula, spread the butter in a thick layer, then sprinkle your chosen flavoring over it. Use the spatula to mix the flavoring into the salt, scraping the salt and folding it over itself several times until the flavoring is mixed evenly into the butter.

3 Scrape the butter into a mound, then transfer it to a piece of plastic wrap. Using your spatula or clean hands, form the butter into a long log, then wrap it tightly in the plastic wrap. Chill for several hours or until firm. To use, cut slices off the log. The butter will keep, wrapped tightly and refrigerated, for 3 to 4 days, or frozen for up to 1 month.

CHAPTER 6

SWEETS ON SALT

Salty and sweet is a classic combination that's been well explored over the past few years. Salt has long been an ingredient, albeit in small quantities, in baked goods, but today you're more likely to find large flakes of sea salt topping your chocolate bonbons, or a more pronounced flavor of salt in your caramel ice cream. There's a reason: Scientists have found that the presence of salt actually increases our perception of sweetness.

If you're a fan of the salty-sweet marriage, you'll love the recipes on the following pages, which play up this pairing.

CARAMELIZED BANANAS WITH RUM-RAISIN MASCARPONE

Carmelized bananas are always a treat, but more so with a touch of salt to enhance their flavor. Make sure to not overwork the mascarpone once you add the rum as it will curdle and break.

SERVES 4

¼ cup raisins

2 tablespoons dark rum, divided

8 ounces mascarpone

2 medium bananas

⅓ cup packed brown sugar

4 shortbread cookies, crumbled

1   Soak the raisins in the dark rum until plump, about an hour. Strain the raisins from the rum, reserving both.

2   Preheat the salt block, beginning with low heat and gradually increasing the temperature to medium-high, until the surface temperature is about 400°F.

3   In a medium bowl, whisk the mascarpone until smooth. Add 1 tablespoon of reserved rum, and stir until just incorporated. Gently fold in the raisins.

4   Slice the bananas on a bias, about 1 inch thick. Place the bananas in a medium bowl and toss with the remaining rum, then coat in brown sugar. Place on the salt block and cook until the bottom is caramelized, about 1½ minutes. Turn and cook until the second side is caramelized, about 1 to 1½ minutes. Remove and divide among four bowls. Top with the rum raisin mascarpone and crumbled shortbread cookies.

SEARED SPICY-SWEET GRAPEFRUIT

After making this recipe, you'll never want to eat plain grapefruit again! This recipe calls for hot paprika, adding a pleasant hint of heat. Simply substitute regular paprika for a milder version. We do not recommend segmenting the grapefruit before cooking as the juices prevent the sugars from caramelizing as nicely.

SERVES 4

2 medium grapefruits
¼ cup packed brown sugar

1 teaspoon smoked paprika
1 teaspoon hot paprika

1 Preheat the salt block on the stove or grill, beginning with low heat and gradually increasing the temperature to medium-high, until the surface temperature is about 400°F.

2 Cut each grapefruit in half. In a small bowl, whisk together the brown sugar, smoked paprika, and hot paprika. Divide half of the sugar mixture among the cut sides of the four grapefruit halves, and spread to coat the flesh.

3 Place the grapefruit halves flesh side down on the salt block, and cook for 1 minute. Wipe the caramelized sugar off the block with each grapefruit half as you remove it.

4 Divide the remaining sugar mixture among the four halves, and reapply to coat the flesh. Place the grapefruit halves sugar side down on the salt block, and cook for another 45 seconds. Wipe the caramelized sugar off the block with each grapefruit half as you remove it. Let cool enough to handle without risk of being burned. Eat with a grapefruit spoon.

COOK'S NOTE

As an alternative, juice the seared grapefruits, add gin, and serve over ice for a kicked-up variation of a Salty Dog cocktail.

RUSTIC RASPBERRY-RHUBARB TART

The marzipan in this recipe adds just the right amount of sweet nuttiness to balance the tartness of the berries and rhubarb, making for a winning flavor combination. Substitute plums, apricots, peaches, or apples in place of the raspberries and rhubarb, depending on what time of year you are making this dessert.

SERVES 8 TO 12

1½ cups all-purpose flour, plus more for dusting

1 stick unsalted butter, chilled

7 ounces chilled marzipan, divided

4–6 tablespoons ice water

12 ounces fresh raspberries

3 stalks rhubarb, chopped

¼ cup packed brown sugar

1 teaspoon orange zest

½ teaspoon cinnamon

2 tablespoons unsalted butter, melted

1 Preheat the oven to 375°F. Preheat the salt block on the stove, beginning with low heat and gradually increasing the temperature to medium-high, until the surface temperature is about 350°F to 375°F. Transfer the hot salt block to the middle rack in the oven.

2 Meanwhile, place the flour in the bowl of a food processor. Cut the butter and half the marzipan into small pieces. Scatter the marzipan evenly over the flour, and pulse three or four times to combine. Do the same with half of the butter, followed by the remaining butter. Add the water to the flour mixture 1 tablespoon at a time, followed by one or two long pulses of the food processor until the dough forms into a ball. Turn out the dough onto a floured work surface, and form into a disk. Cover with plastic wrap, and refrigerate for about 30 minutes.

3 Add the raspberries, rhubarb, brown sugar, orange zest, and cinnamon to a bowl and toss to combine. Set aside.

4 On a well-floured work surface, adding additional flour as needed to prevent sticking, roll out the dough to about 12 inches in diameter. Slice the remaining marzipan into ⅛-inch-thick rounds, create a circle so they touch, and roll out with a rolling pin to approximately a 6-inch round. Place the marzipan in the center of the dough, leaving about a 2½- to 3-inch border at the edges. Spread the raspberry-rhubarb mixture evenly

over the marzipan, and pour the juices over the top. Fold the edges of the dough over the fruit. Brush the dough and top with the melted butter.

5 Carefully transfer the tart to the hot salt block. Place the salt block on a baking rack set in a sheet pan in order to catch any juices that may run off, and bake until the crust is golden brown, about 45 minutes. Cool for 5 minutes before serving with vanilla bean ice cream or fresh whipped cream.

COOK'S NOTE

You will want to make certain the dough is not sticking to your work surface before spreading the fruit and forming the tart. We suggest working on a flat cookie sheet or pizza peel that will allow for an easier transfer to the hot salt block. Be sure to mend any tears in your dough, as it is preferable to minimize the juices dripping onto the salt block.

PEANUT BUTTER–HONEY COOKIES

Peanut butter and honey is such a nostalgic flavor combination, and it really plays well with salt in this recipe. As we found out when soliciting feedback for this recipe, soft versus crisp is a divisive characteristic in peanut butter cookies, so please note that these land squarely in the soft category.

MAKES APPROXIMATELY 32 COOKIES

1½ cups all-purpose flour

1 teaspoon baking powder

1 cup creamy peanut butter

1 stick unsalted butter, room temperature

½ cup packed brown sugar

¼ cup honey

1 Preheat the oven to 375°F. Preheat the salt block on the stove, beginning with low heat and gradually increasing the temperature to medium-high, until the surface temperature is about 350°F. Transfer the hot salt block to the middle rack in the oven.

2 In a small bowl, whisk together the flour and baking powder.

3 In the bowl of a stand mixer, cream together the peanut butter and butter until thoroughly combined. Add the brown sugar and honey, and continue to mix until the sugar is completely incorporated. Slowly add the flour mixture, and mix until combined.

4 Using a tablespoon, scoop the dough and roll into a ball. Place on the hot salt block, and gently flatten with the back of a fork, creating a crosshatch pattern. Repeat, spacing the cookies about ½ inch apart. You will get about 12 cookies on the block.

5 Bake for 10 minutes, until golden brown. Remove from the oven, let the cookies rest for 1 minute, and then transfer to wire racks to cool. Repeat until you've used up the remaining dough, approximately 2 additional batches.

BROWN SUGAR AND SEA SALT SHORTBREAD

When a cookie has only a few ingredients, quality matters. I like to use the best quality butter I can find for these simple but sophisticated little cookies. My favorite is Plugrá or another similar European-style butter.

MAKES 16 COOKIES

2 sticks unsalted butter, room temperature

½ cup packed brown sugar

1 teaspoon vanilla bean paste (see cook's note)

2¼ cups all-purpose flour, plus more for dusting

2 tablespoons cornstarch

1–2 teaspoons flaky sea salt, as needed

1 Preheat the oven to 325°F. Preheat the salt block on the stove, beginning with low heat and gradually increasing the temperature to medium-high, until the surface temperature is 325°F. Transfer the hot salt block to the middle rack in the oven.

2 Meanwhile, in the bowl of a stand mixer, cream together the butter, brown sugar, and vanilla. In a mixing bowl, whisk together the flour and cornstarch. Add the flour mixture to the butter mixture, and mix on low speed just until combined. The dough will be very crumbly.

3 Turn the dough out onto a lightly floured surface, and pat into a rectangle, about 6 inches by 8 inches, about ½ inch thick. Use a pizza cutter or a bench scraper to cut the dough in half lengthwise, then each half into eight fingers.

4 Remove the hot salt block from the oven, quickly arrange the pieces on the block, and sprinkle with sea salt. Return to the oven, and bake for 25 to 30 minutes, until golden.

COOK'S NOTE

Vanilla bean paste is made of vanilla bean seeds and pods and is available in the baking or spice department of specialty food stores. You can also use an actual vanilla bean: Split the pod in half lengthwise and scrape out the tiny seeds inside. If you don't get a full teaspoon of seeds, that's okay.

SALTED BUTTERSCOTCH PUDDING

A judicious dose of salt accentuates the mellow caramel flavor of butterscotch. This recipe calls for mixing the pudding on a chilled salt block, which stirs in just enough of the salt flavor. You can also serve dollops of pudding right on the salt block for a lovely presentation.

SERVES 4

1 cup packed brown sugar

¼ cup cornstarch

¼ teaspoon salt

2½ cups whole milk

½ cup heavy cream

3 egg yolks

3 tablespoons unsalted butter, cut into pieces

1 teaspoon vanilla extract

1   Place the salt block in the refrigerator to chill for several hours or overnight.

2   Place the brown sugar, cornstarch, and salt in a saucepan, preferably one with rounded sides. Whisk to combine and to break up any lumps in the sugar. Over medium heat, whisk in the milk and cream. Stirring frequently with the whisk, bring to a simmer. Reduce heat to medium-low to maintain the simmer and cook for 1 minute or until thickened, stirring frequently.

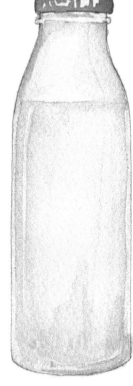

3   In a metal mixing bowl, whisk the egg yolks. Add a few tablespoonfuls of the hot milk mixture to the eggs, and whisk to combine. Continue whisking in milk, gradually, a few spoonfuls at a time, to heat the egg mixture until the outside of the bowl feels very warm. Pour the egg mixture into the saucepan, and whisk to combine. Bring to a simmer and, stirring constantly, cook for 1 minute, until thickened. Remove from the heat, and stir in the butter and vanilla. Transfer to a shallow dish, cover with plastic wrap, and refrigerate until cool.

4   Just before serving, place ¾-cup dollops on the chilled salt block. Serve by scooping up a dollop with two rubber spatulas and placing it in a dessert bowl. Mix before eating to make sure the salt flavor is evenly dispersed.

SALTED PECAN TURTLES

Being denizens of the South, we're big fans of all things pecan, and these turtles remind us of the goodies from one of our favorite local candy makers. Not a fan of pecans? Walnuts, pistachios, peanuts, or almonds would all be delicious variations.

MAKES ABOUT 2 DOZEN CANDIES

1 cup granulated sugar

½ cup packed brown sugar

1 stick unsalted butter

½ cup whole milk

½ cup heavy cream

¼ cup light corn syrup

1 cup semisweet chocolate chips

2 cups toasted pecan halves

1 Chill the salt block for several hours or overnight.

2 In a heavy saucepan, combine the granulated sugar, brown sugar, butter, milk, cream, and corn syrup. Bring to a boil, and reduce the heat to maintain a simmer. Cook, stirring occasionally, for around 15 minutes, until the bubbles are thicker and slower to pop. You can test the caramel by dropping a little into a cup of ice water. It should form a ball that is chewy but still soft.

3 While the caramel is cooking, melt the chocolate chips in a small saucepan or in the microwave.

4 Use a spoon to spread the chocolate into thin circles, about 1 inch in diameter on the salt block. Arrange the pecans in groups of two or three on top of each round of chocolate. Working quickly, before the caramel hardens, spoon about 1 tablespoon of caramel over each cluster of pecans. When the caramel sets a little, spoon a dollop of chocolate (about 1 tablespoon or less) on top of each, spreading it to cover most of the caramel. (Conversely, you can eliminate the base of chocolate and arrange the pecans in clusters directly on the salt block, spooning the caramel and chocolate over them.) Place the salt block in the refrigerator for several hours, until the chocolate hardens. The caramel can be gently rewarmed over low heat if you need to make a second batch. When the candy is set, use a metal offset spatula to remove from the salt block.

CHERRY-MARSHMALLOW CHOCOLATE "KISSES"

This pretty confection takes a little effort, but the results are well worth it. We like to box these and give them as a hostess gift, a present for a teacher, or a thank-you for a pet sitter. If you prefer a different flavor, you can substitute strawberry, raspberry, or another flavor of your choice for the cherry. You can find flavoring oils at cake supply stores or craft stores with a cake decorating department. The brand we use is LorAnn Oils.

MAKES ABOUT 2 DOZEN "KISSES"

2 envelopes gelatin

⅔ cup cold water, divided

1½ cups granulated sugar

⅔ cup light corn syrup

pinch of salt

2 teaspoons vanilla extract

½ teaspoon cherry flavor

red food coloring, as needed

12 ounces semisweet chocolate chips

ghee, as needed

½ cup powdered sugar

1 Chill the salt block for several hours or overnight.

2 In the bowl of a stand mixer, combine the gelatin and ⅓ cup of cold water. Stir to moisten the gelatin, and set aside.

3 In a medium saucepan over medium-high heat, combine the sugar, corn syrup, salt, and the remaining ⅓ cup of cold water. Cook, stirring frequently, until melted. Bring to a simmer and cook, without stirring, until the sugar mixture registers 235°F on a candy thermometer. This will take about 5 to 7 minutes.

3 With the whisk attachment on the stand mixer, run the mixer on low speed and gradually pour the sugar mixture in a steady stream into the gelatin. Gradually increase the speed to high, and beat until the mixture is white, looks glossy, and forms stiff peaks, about 12 to 15 minutes. Add the vanilla, the cherry flavor, and a few drops of red food coloring (enough to tint the marshmallow mixture pink), and beat for 30 seconds more to combine.

4 While the marshmallow is being mixed, melt the chocolate chips in the microwave or on the stove. Rub a light coating of ghee over the chilled salt block to prevent the chocolate from sticking. Then use a spoon to spread the chocolate into thin circles, about 1 inch in diameter.

5 Scrape the marshmallow mixture into a disposable plastic pastry bag, and cut about 1 inch off the tip. Pipe a dollop of marshmallow mixture on top of each chocolate circle. Shake or sift powdered sugar over the candies. Refrigerate the salt block until the candies are set, 2 to 3 hours. Use a metal spatula or scraper if needed to remove the candies from the salt block.

APPENDIX

SALT BLOCK SOURCES

Charcoal Companion

The most mainstream supplier of Himalayan salt blocks.

www.companion-group.com/brands/charcoal-companion/

800-521-0505

Cost Plus World Market

A source of affordable salt blocks and holders.

www.worldmarket.com

877-967-5362

Crate & Barrel

A good source for salt blocks and holders.

www.crateandbarrel.com

800-967-6696

Home Depot

Razor blade scrapers, thermometers, salt blocks, and more.

www.homedepot.com

800-466-3337

Salt Rox

A salt block manufacturer selling blocks treated with a proprietary process to make them more durable.

www.saltrox.com

859-351-8160

The Meadow

A retailer with locations in Portland, Oregon, and New York City, as well as online, selling a variety of Himalayan salt blocks and related products.

www.atthemeadow.com

503-305-3388

Sur la Table

Salt blocks of various sizes, plus holders and storage totes.

www.surlatable.com

800-243-0852

Williams-Sonoma

A variety of Himalayan salt blocks and accessories, including holders and a rack to turn your salt block into a grill press.

www.williams-sonoma.com

877-812-6235

WHAT TO DO WITH YOUR SPENT SALT BLOCK

As a Seasoning

- Use a fine grater, such as a Microplane, to grate it into small granules to use as finishing salt.

- Break the salt block into small pieces and add them to a salt grinder.

- Break into chunks, about 1 inch in diameter, and drop into water boiling for pasta, potatoes, or vegetables. Boil for around 2 minutes, then remove the chunk and save for another use before adding the food being cooked.

- Dissolve a few chunks from a salt block in warm water, add some herbs, and use as a brine for chicken or turkey.

In the Bath

Grind the salt block into fine pieces with a grater or a hammer. Add a handful to the bath or, if the pieces are fine enough, combine with olive oil and a few drops of an essential oil like lavender or peppermint for fragrance, and use as a body scrub.

CONVERSION CHARTS

Volume Conversions

U.S.	U.S. Equivalent	Metric
1 tablespoon (3 teaspoons)	½ fluid ounce	15 milliliters
¼ cup	2 fluid ounces	60 milliliters
⅓ cup	3 fluid ounces	90 milliliters
½ cup	4 fluid ounces	120 milliliters
⅔ cup	5 fluid ounces	150 milliliters
¾ cup	6 fluid ounces	180 milliliters
1 cup	8 fluid ounces	240 milliliters
2 cups	16 fluid ounces	480 milliliters

Weight Conversions

U.S.	Metric
½ ounce	15 grams
1 ounce	30 grams
2 ounces	60 grams
¼ pound	115 grams
⅓ pound	150 grams
½ pound	225 grams
¾ pound	350 grams
1 pound	450 grams

Temperature Conversions

Fahrenheit (°F)	Celsius (°C)
200°F	95°C
225°F	110°C
250°F	120°C
275°F	135°C
300°F	150°C
325°F	165°C
350°F	175°C
375°F	190°C
400°F	200°C
425°F	220°C
450°F	230°C

INDEX

ACKNOWLEDGMENTS

Jessica and Kelley wish to acknowledge the support and teamwork of the Ulysses Press staff, particularly Alice Riegert, Kourtney Joy, and Susan Lang. We'd also like to thank our families for their continued faith in us and willingness to be taste testers and dish washers.

ABOUT THE AUTHORS

JESSICA GOLDBOGEN HARLAN has written about food and cooking for more than 20 years. A graduate of the Institute of Culinary Education, she also works as a caterer and does cooking classes and demos for children and adults. Her previous books include *Ramen to the Rescue*, *Tortillas to the Rescue*, *Crazy for Breakfast Sandwiches*, *Homemade Condiments*, and *Quinoa Cuisine* (cowritten with Kelley Sparwasser). She lives in Atlanta with her husband and two daughters.

KELLEY SPARWASSER spent her early years glued to her grandmother's hip while her grandmother cooked at the stove. After graduating from Stephens College, she completed the Culinary Arts program at Clark College and cooked at restaurants in Portland, Oregon. She then moved to New York City where she worked on the editorial staffs of *McCall's* and the esteemed hospitality industry trade magazine, *Food Arts*, before returning to Portland to work at a winery in the Willamette Valley. She relocated to Atlanta with her husband and works for a prominent restaurant group. Kelley and Jessica are the co-authors of *Quinoa Cuisine*, published by Ulysses Press in 2012.

CPSIA information can be obtained
at www.ICGtesting.com
Printed in the USA
LVHW020053051121
702486LV00004B/8